QuickStart
Circumnavigation Guide

PROVEN ROUTE AND
SAILING ITINERARY
TIMED FOR WEATHER

Captain Charlie & Cathy Simon

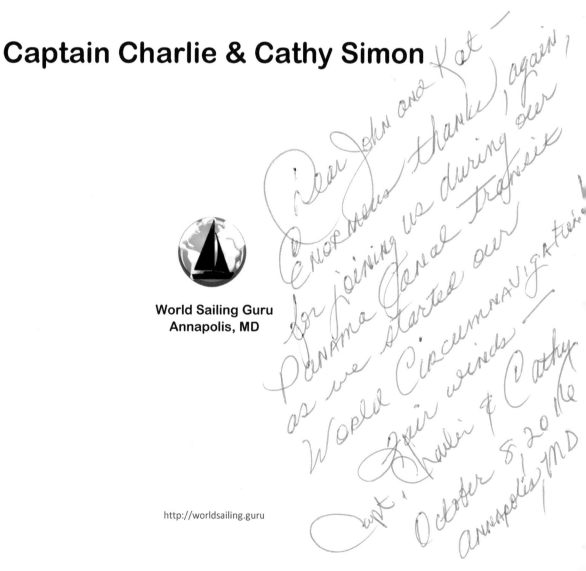

World Sailing Guru
Annapolis, MD

http://worldsailing.guru

Dear John and Kat —
Enormous thanks, again,
for joining us during our
Panama Canal Transit
as we started our
World Circumnavigation.

Fair winds,
Capt. Charlie & Cathy
October 8, 2016
Annapolis, MD

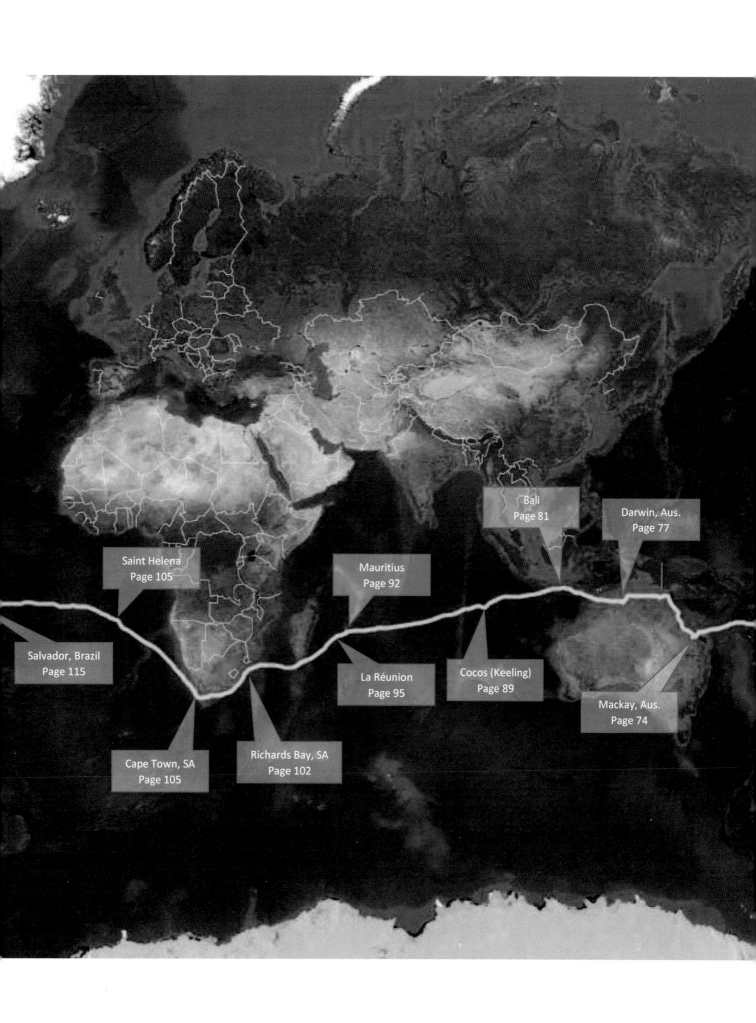

Bali
Page 81

Darwin, Aus.
Page 77

Saint Helena
Page 105

Mauritius
Page 92

Salvador, Brazil
Page 115

La Réunion
Page 95

Cocos (Keeling)
Page 89

Mackay, Aus.
Page 74

Cape Town, SA
Page 105

Richards Bay, SA
Page 102

Acknowledgments

A special acknowledgment to Captain Joshua Slocum and his sailboat *Spray* who famously sailed around the world before us. Also, we applaud Jimmy Cornell who began leading a rally of sailboats around the world and the World Cruising Club's World ARC Rally for continuing to assist sailors to sail the oceans.

Several people in particular inspired our voyage. We met Kay LeClaire at a friend's wedding. Kay had recently climbed Mount Everest at age 60. Also, Cathy met Pat Henry some months later who was one of the first women to sail a solo circumnavigation. Pat is a recipient of the Joshua Slocum Society's International Golden Circle Award.

Never failing in his encouragement to us was Richard Spindler, publisher of *Latitude 38* in San Francisco; whether it was what boat we should choose or generously writing about us sailing.

So many, many thanks to David Walters at David Walters Yachts for all the care taken in finding our sailboat, *Celebrate*; and to Stuart Dodd of Global Marine Services for extensive preparation of *Celebrate* for the trip.

Enormous thanks to our crew of family and friends for joining us on various legs of the journey: Steve Simon (from Florida to Saint Lucia, West Indies), Andy Barrow (from Saint Lucia to Panama), John and Kat Langenheim (Panama Canal transit), Peter Sandover (Indian Ocean), and Jay Ailworth (South Atlantic Ocean).

Very special thanks to our wonderful friends who traveled so far to be at our send-off from Saint Lucia: Dr. John and Priscilla Cadwell, Dr. David and Rebecca Egger, Stacey and Anne Cowles, and Don and Charlotte Lamp.

Huge thanks to other family and friends who sailed with us over the years: Jay Woods, the Michelle McDowell Lobdell family, the Culbertson family, Ken Bertino, Chris and Patti Wuerz, John Ashburn, Greg Retkowski, Cherie Sogsti, Laurie Ailworth, and Linda Frakes.

For special kindnesses along the way: Andrew Bishop, Paul and Suzana Tetlow, Joel Chadwick, Martine Waitt, Chris Tibbs, Hugh Murray-Walker, Jonny Buraca, Jeremy Wyatt, Sarah Collins, Lyall Burgess, Peter Burch, Mia Karlsson, John and Joyce Easteal, Jonathan and Jenny Crowe, Christoph and Dagmar Hartung, the Ramsey family, Jean-Thomas and Sandra Frank, Hubert Hirschfeld, Wolf Fassbender, Siegfried Hahn, Silvano Sighinolfi, Vittorio Setti, Jan Mar, the Kleiberg family, Lauren Wargo, Brian Sears, Jan Sanberger and Irina Micheilis, Sheila (Polaris) Rietscher, Doña de Mallorca, Leon Ablon and Dixie Piver, Cameron Freeman, Brian O'Grady, the Ivanissevich family, Edward Jaschek, the Haufe family, the Stokes family, the Hagon family, Nuno Simas, Tom Toohey, James Reinhard, Alex Hernandez, Markus Witschi, Gaetano Arezzo, Ralf Jager, the Fox family, the Heyne family, the Owen family, Eric Taveau, the Ryder family, Vlado Porvaznik, Konrad Zeller, Achim Haller, Finn Porteous, Peter Shoosmith, Heather Sutton, Jeanine Miami, Don Desmond, Frank Sluka, the Robinson family, Bob and Julia Fairchild, Shelly Willard, KC Fullmer, Ryan Newland, Molly Winans, Mark Brownhill, Eric Sorensen, Erica Curless, Kate Spencer, Bob Frantz, Jim Dean, the Powell family, the Birnbaum family, Ellen Low, Darlene Bos, Cheri Hanes, the Murray family, the Barrett family, Susi Walsh, Phil and Jane Johnson, Dr. Elizabeth Welty, the Kaya family, Robyn Tucker, Jack Heath, Keith Woodland, Bill Simer, Eckart Preu, Liz Barrow, Linda Miller Sheets, Willemina Van Pelt, Veronica Speigl, Jane Sandover, Chris Schnug, Chris Jerome, Philippa Morgan, Andrea Mia Apollo, Alison Gieschen, Mona Boyle, the Thompson family, the Kennedy family, and the Simon family.

Also, sincere thanks to the following organizations which have helped us to encourage sailing: Sail Nauticus/Nauticus National Maritime Center, National Sailing Hall of Fame, Corinthian Yacht Club of San Francisco, Seven Seas University, Ocean Cruising Club, US Sailing Organization, Annapolis Yacht Club Foundation, Vallarta Yacht Club, *WSU Magazine*, and *SpinSheet*.

Watermark photo by Jay Ailworth.

QuickStart
Circumnavigation
Guide

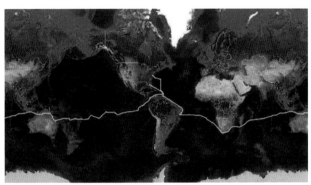

Satellite tracking route of Captain Charlie Simon and his wife, Cathy Simon.

"The wonderful sea charmed me from the first."
—*Captain Joshua Slocum*

Table of Contents

We Want to Hear from You!

Your comments, suggestions, and corrections are invited. We appreciate hearing from anyone who finds errors in this publication. We are interested in ideas about what you would like in future editions of the QuickStart *Circumnavigation Guide*. There are a number of members of the World Sailing Guru community who contribute to our website. Our readers are interested in *your* experiences and tips as well. We post cruising reports, pictures, videos, updates about changes in specified areas, and tips that range from anchoring to restaurants to technical issues. Contact us through our website, by mail, or by e-mail.

Caution: This book was designed to provide experienced skippers with cruising information about the waters covered. While great effort has been taken to make the QuickStart *Circumnavigation Guide* complete and accurate, it is possible that oversights, differences of interpretation, and factual errors will be found. Thus, none of the information contained in the book is warranted to be accurate or appropriate for any specific need. Furthermore, variations in weather and sea conditions, a mariner's skills and experience, and the presence of luck (good or bad) can dictate a mariner's proper course of action.

The QuickStart *Circumnavigation Guide* should be viewed as a reference only and not a substitute for official government charts, tide and current tables, coast pilots, sailing directions, and local notices to mariners. The QuickStart *Circumnavigation Guide* assumes the user to be law-abiding and of good will. The suggestions offered are not all-inclusive but are meant to help avoid unpleasantness or needless delay.

The publisher, editors, and authors assume no liability for errors or omissions, or for any loss or damages incurred from using the publication.

Printed in the United States of America.

ISBN: 1530491975
ISBN 13: 9781530491971

Library of Congress Control Number: 2016908305
CreateSpace Independent Publishing Platform, North Charleston, SC

Printing Version: 6/20/16

Book Sales, worldwide:
> **Amazon**, other retail outlets, and distributed through **Ingram**.

E-books at:
> http://circumnavigationguide.com

Other Contacts:
> info@worldsailing.guru
> http://worldsailing.guru

 Like us on Facebook at
http://facebook.com/worldsailingguru

QuickStart
CIRCUMNAVIGATION
GUIDE

Publisher's Cataloging-in-Publication
(Provided by Quality Books, Inc.)

Simon, Charles J., author.
    Quickstart circumnavigation guide : proven route and sailing itinerary timed for weather / Charlie & Cathy Simon.
    pages cm
    Includes bibliographical references and index.
    LCCN 2016908305
    ISBN 9781530491971

    1. Voyages around the world. 2. Sailing.
I. Simon, Cathy, author. II. Title.

G420.S5696Q53 2016   910.4'1
                  QBI16-600083

Author's Perspective

"As sailors, we get to experience places that cannot be seen by traveling on land or by air."

—Captain Charlie Simon
BSEE, MSCS

After sailing to Alaska twice; cruising the west coast of Canada, the United States, Mexico, and Central America; and then transiting the Panama Canal to begin cruising the Bahamas, the East Coast of the United States and up to Nova Scotia, it was time to do a world circumnavigation!

I have been sailing most of my life, and when I married Cathy nearly 40 years ago, she joined in my enthusiasm. As a child, I learned to sail from my father, who had been a longtime San Francisco Bay sailor. He recounted stories of sailing on Commodore Piver's 86-foot schooner *Eloise* from the 1930s onward.

After owning two other sailboats, we purchased our current boat, *Celebrate*, a Taswell 58, for our circumnavigation. Following nearly a year of improvements to make our voyage as safe and comfortable as possible, we arrived in Saint Lucia in the West Indies for the start of the World ARC 2014–15.

Captain Charlie Simon avoiding icebergs at Tracy Arm in southeast Alaska.

We both learned so much on the world trip that we felt the need to encourage others—hence this book. No matter what your sailing experience, you return from any substantial sailing trip with improved abilities and more knowledge and experience than when you started out.

We wish you happy sailing and hope you will have safe, comfortable voyages!

What's New about This Book

"Sailing around the world is a life-changing experience."

—Cathy Simon
BA

This is the book I wish we'd had when we began to prepare for our world circumnavigation. This book is here to encourage you to get started with your own world cruise. It shows you an easy way to begin—by following a proven route and itinerary that are timed for weather to maximize safety and comfort.

We have a whole shelf of cruising guides and ocean-sailing instructional books, and the sheer amount of information can be overwhelming. By having a given itinerary, you have a starting point for planning or deciding how to adjust your calendar to fit your own cruising style.

Cathy Simon collecting "bergy bits" in Glacier Bay, Alaska.

The key issue: to start cruising, you have to leave the dock. This book describes requirements for equipping a boat and for educating yourself and your crew so you can cast off.

We highly recommend getting additional guides as well, as they offer many details which can extend the knowledge contained here. There is a suggested guide list on page 162. Our *QuickStart* guide shows the primary stops that many cruisers make. Cruising guides for individual areas offer more options and more detail.

If you're an experienced day sailor and/or coastal cruiser, this book builds on your experience to help you get started on your "Adventure of a Lifetime" with helpful tips as well as suggestions for great places to visit and many things you can do to make your trip as enjoyable as possible.

How to Cruise the World in a Sailboat: The Adventure of a Lifetime!

A circumnavigation following the trade winds takes you to some of the best cruising grounds in the world. From the Panama Canal, through the Pacific, Indian, and south Atlantic Oceans, and back to the Caribbean side of the Panama Canal is about 26,000 nautical miles (nm). Along the way are spectacular sights and impressive cities, too, including Panama City at the Panama Canal, and Cape Town, South Africa, with every amenity imaginable. It is a journey of endless possibilities, amazing destinations, outstanding wildlife, wonderful people, and a whole range of opportunities for sailing and stopping. You can choose where you want to go, when, and for how long. Also, you can choose your cruising style—from the minimalist to the posh.

As you choose your itinerary, you can fit it to your own needs and interests. Whether you are an amateur naturalist, a sociologist, an artist, a photographer, or an all-out sailing competitive racer, you'll be able to fulfill your dreams while sailing around the world.

A Spectacular Stop

Fiji Islands, a perfect place! When we sailed around the world, finishing in 2015, one of our absolute favorite cruising places was Fiji. With more than 300 islands, there are plenty of choices of idyllic stops. On a boat meandering between islands, the distances are reasonable, and most of the waters are reef-protected with only a few longer, open-water passages. Anchorages are plentiful.

Fiji natives. Photo courtesy of Tourism Fiji.

Wildlife is outstanding! Whales are regularly spotted. Birds are everywhere. Dolphins, sharks, rays, rainbow coral, sea stars, and a myriad of other sea life call Fiji home.

Beautiful Fiji, underwater. Photo by FrontierOfficial (License CC-BY-2.0).

Natural beauty is everywhere! The volcanic peaks of the Yasawa group are visible in the chain of about 20 islands. These are famous for crystal-blue lagoons (and were the site chosen for filming the movie *Blue Lagoon*), white sandy beaches, and lush tropical rainforests. Fiji's rainforests are unique because they have no harmful animals or insects. There are numerous waterfalls; the most famous to visit being the sacred Bouma Falls on the island of Taveuni.

Cruising Choices

In choosing your mode of sailing, you can start by asking yourself, "How much time do I have?" On their own, few people circumnavigate in fewer than three years, and many take five to ten years. To go around in fewer than two years, consider joining a rally. This will lighten your planning load and speed up the process of check-in at each country you visit. Organized tours at each destination can help you get an overview of each country before visiting a few places on your own.

Another important question is, "Do I want to do all this myself?" You may single-hand, sail with just your spouse, bring on additional family or crew, or hire a professional captain.

You may elect to skip long blue-water passages and simply fly to wonderful destinations and charter a boat. Charter fleets are plentiful in many of the best cruising areas.

S/V Celebrate *in the South Pacific. Photo by Folie a Deux.*

Do you have the boat already, or do you plan to purchase one for the trip? For offshore cruising, a blue-water ocean-voyaging vessel is ideal. A good offshore cruising boat is strongly built and seaworthy. Most offshore cruising boats (even with just a couple aboard) are now a minimum of 40 feet ranging up to 50 feet—large enough to be comfortable but small enough to be handled by two people. No matter what your boat, you'll want to allot at least a year for outfitting prior to departure.

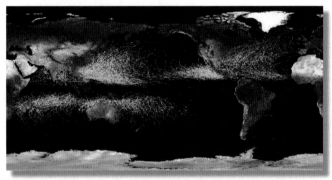

This NASA chart of historical hurricane/cyclone tracks emphasizes that there are "safer" areas to travel. Hurricanes can usually be avoided completely by sailing in hurricane-prone areas in winter months only.

Choosing Your Route: Trade Winds, Cyclones, and Currents

The key to a safe and comfortable world cruise is to choose routes and timing for the best possible sailing conditions. Choosing the safest and most comfortable route around the world depends largely on the weather. Most cruisers choose warmer climates, sailing downwind, avoiding seasonal areas of storms and hurricanes ("cyclones" in the Southern Hemisphere, "typhoons" in Asia), and using current boosts when possible. By looking at the probabilities of

good conditions, it is possible to select a route for the safest and most comfortable sailing experience.

The article "QuickStart to Choosing Your Route and Timing," on page 149, describes how a route can be selected that follows prevailing winds and minimizes the risks of seasonal storms.

As you can see, the enormous variety of experiences, the breathtaking vistas, and the wonder of wildlife keep us cruising.

Blue-Water Sailing

Even if you are an experienced sailor, the around-the-world trip is different from a day sail on the bay in fundamental ways. While planning your adventure, be sure to consider all the following:

- Passages are longer. This means you need greater capacities for everything (food, water, fuel, spares, etc.).
- You are further from shore. You won't have access to towing services or coast guard rescues. You'll need to be more self-sufficient and carry more safety equipment.
- You'll be sailing 24/7. This is harder on equipment and crew. You'll need backups.
- Half of your sailing will be at night. Be sure you have the skills and lights to reef at night and take care of the inevitable breakage in the dark.
- You'll sometimes get worse weather. You'll have some passages which span more time than the best weather prediction.
- Be prepared for rougher conditions. You'll likely encounter sea states that might keep you at the dock if you weren't already at sea.
- You'll be in close quarters aboard. You can go for afternoon races with six on a 40-foot boat with just about anyone. On a long ocean passage, even the best of friends may have their relationships strained. It is best if you clearly define your expectations for your crew and write them down.
- You may be shorthanded. You'll want to rig your boat so your on-watch crew (often only one person) can reef without waking the rest of the crew.
- Plan your maintenance budget. Instead of considering what you've been spending per year on your boat, consider your cost per sailing hour. Then you can be pleasantly surprised instead of shocked.

Top Ideas

This section includes some of the most useful items we added to our boat before our departure.

Engine and Fuel: If you have light winds or if the wind dies completely, which it usually does in the ITCZ (Intertropical Convergence Zone, or doldrums), you'll need a good engine and ample fuel capacity. The "Itinerary Sample" and "Port Services Summary" (pages 135 and 136) can be useful in calculating the fuel capacity you'll want for longer passages.

Full Cockpit Enclosure: The weather can be cool and wet, and a full cockpit enclosure, or surround, can be a real comfort item (see photo). A bimini is an absolute must for protection from the tropical sun.

Our cockpit enclosure kept us warm and dry in rough or rainy conditions.

GPS and chart plotters are invaluable for navigation, but be aware that electronic navigation is only as good as the electronic charts. In many places in the world (such as Fiji), many charts are not accurate. Charts have usually been upgraded where ships operate, but in outer islands, you'll need to read the water. Purchase your electronic charts before you depart; you may not be able to get them in a reasonable time outside your home country.

Use Google Maps or Google Earth as additional aids to navigation. You probably won't have the bandwidth during passages, so before you leave, you can use these services to preload images or check waypoints to your destination. For details, see the section on page 151.

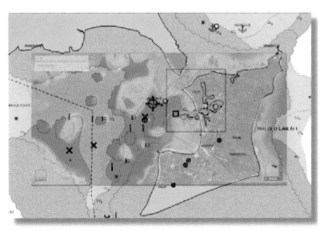

In some instances, a look at Google Earth can help to provide locations for reefs. Here (at Musket Cove, Fiji), the nautical chart (the larger image) is overlaid on Google Earth to illustrate the discrepancy between charted and photographed reef positions.

Radar: We upgraded to the best color radar we could install. Not only is radar useful in times of limited visibility, but you'll also be able to use it to track squalls (to know better when to reef). Also, if you overlay a radar display on the

chart plotter, it can show how well the chart aligns with actual landforms and aids to navigation.

AIS: In my mind, an AIS transponder is a must. With a receiver, you can see ships approaching up to 20 miles away. With the transponder, they can see you, and you'll be able to watch them alter course to avoid you.

> **IMPORTANT**: AIS and radar do not relieve you from keeping a good lookout. You'll find local fishing boats many miles offshore, and they probably don't carry AIS, may not have much of a radar echo, and may not even have lights.

Substantial Ground Tackle: In our shakedown test, our anchor would drag in a 35- to 40-knot wind, so we upgraded to a larger main anchor. Anchoring depths where we went were seldom over 50 feet, but we carry at least 300 feet of chain as a safety measure. In anchorages near coral, all chain is necessary as coral will cut rope rode.

Dinghies and Tenders: A convenient dinghy launching and recovery system is important. When anchored or tied to a mooring buoy, you'll need your dinghy to travel ashore. Cruisers use their dinghies extensively for exploring and fishing, and they can also be considered important safety equipment. We have friends who have used their dinghy to push their boat into a port after their main engine failed.

Permanently Rigged Preventers: You'll be sailing downwind much of the time, and a preventer keeps the boom from slamming across in the event of an accidental jibe. We prefer a permanent installation so the preventer is there when you need it. The very conditions that demand a preventer make it very difficult to rig. We have a preventer rigged on each side and led to the cockpit. Some cruisers prefer a boom brake to accomplish the same thing.

Safety Equipment: You'll need a full inventory of flares, flotation, and first-aid items. Follow the recommended list on page 157, and don't scrimp. Many items can be found on eBay or similar sites and can be resold when you return. Additionally, we installed a Watch Commander—a timer that would beep at a preset interval (such as every 15 minutes) to keep the helmsman alert. He then has one minute to press the reset button or the siren blares to signal that the helmsman has gone overboard (or is napping).

Satellite Tracking: We used a YellowBrick satellite tracking unit that is the size of a satellite phone. Not only can it create tracking images, such as the one on the cover of this book, but it can be used for emergency messaging, blogging, and a host of other purposes.

Clothing: Layering clothing works well. Foul-weather gear is essential, including rubber boots.

Helpful Publications: We carry as many cruising guides as we can fit, each offering a different point of view. See the list of cruising guides we used on page 162.

Skills to Hone

Long-distance cruising requires a specific skill set. Of course, you'll need sailing expertise, but here are some additional abilities you'll need to be safe on a longer trip.

Anchoring Technique: Some of the best places to visit are not accessible via a dock. You'll need to anchor in areas that are sometimes less than ideal, and your technique can help make up for poor holding. Most importantly, choose your anchoring location to stay clear of other boats, use sufficient scope, back down your anchor, and consider the impact of changes in wind and current on your anchor and your boat's swing.

Communications at Sea: You'll need to be comfortable with your VHF for local communications, but you'll also need to be familiar with using your shortwave radio (SSB) to participate in longer-range cruiser nets. Practice with your shortwave on a coastal trip before you need it for longer distances.

E-mail at Sea: E-mail can be invaluable, not only for staying in touch but for receiving weather updates. Install a Pactor modem for your SSB, and subscribe to SailMail or a similar service. Back this up with a satellite phone. Neither the SSB nor the satellite phone will work all the time, but with both we could almost always receive a current weather GRIB file when we wanted one.

Electronic Seamanship: You'll be relying on your electronic navigation. Take a class, or make sure you are proficient in all aspects of using your onboard electronics for navigation and communications.

Heavy Weather: If you're not good at reefing at the beginning of your trip, you *will* be by the end. Make sure you have the necessary rigging for easy reefing so you can build your skills.

About Food and Provisioning

Consider that wherever you go, the people living there eat. Accordingly, when you sail the world, food will be available wherever you make landfall. In addition, you can catch fish when you are at sea.

In the highly developed areas, such as Tahiti, Australia, and Cape Town, you'll find supermarkets that rival anything you'll find in the United States. That being said, if you embark on a world cruise with the expectation of eating like an American, you'll probably have a difficult time. Consider stocking up on your favorite nonperishables before you cast off, and modify your food expectations to match local availability and the limitations of cruising.

First off, you'll be embarking on some long passages (up to three weeks), and any expectation of fresh fruit and vegetables over that period of time will be difficult to meet. At least at the end of such a voyage, you will be relying on preserved food: canned, frozen, or dried. You'll also be limited by storage available, especially refrigerator/freezer space. Loading up for a several-week voyage involves loading what seems to be a huge amount of food on board.

When you visit smaller islands or less-developed countries, you'll encounter different food-shopping experiences. A store with a "Supermarket" sign may be the size of a 7-Eleven and have very little fresh food at all. The nearby "market" will have wonderful fresh fruits and vegetables, which you should approach with a little bit of understanding.

Relative to a US supermarket:

- Supplies will be variable, depending on what is available locally or has recently been imported. Ferries might arrive only weekly or monthly to restock the store.
- You'll probably encounter items you've never seen before.
- Food is generally ripe (or overripe), and shelf lives after purchase will be shorter. Even with refrigeration, you might have only a few days before food begins to spoil.
- Food will often be more flavorful but might be less cosmetically attractive. Some of the worst-looking oranges might taste the best.
- Packaged and frozen foods might be substantially more expensive.
- Fresh foods should be washed carefully to avoid possible contamination.

No matter where you are, you can probably get staple items: rice, eggs, flour, dairy products, and a bit of frozen meat.

As food selection can be a very personal issue, cruisers address provisioning issues differently. Here are some strategies:

We like to carry a substantial supply of staples: pasta, packaged fruits, vegetables, some canned meats, and so on. That way, when we go shopping, it can be entertaining rather than a necessity. We can go food shopping, explore, try new items, and know that we won't go hungry if the food shopping doesn't work out.

Consider the possibility of going to your local 7-Eleven with a requirement of purchasing food for six people for two weeks. This gives you the idea of what could be the situation on small islands, where virtually everything is brought in by the occasional freighter. If you arrive before the freighter is due, your options will be significantly limited, and various canned foods could seem preferable to the remaining store stock.

Some cruisers rely entirely on locally available food. We also know some cruisers who stocked dehydrated meals sufficient for most of their voyage.

Should You Join a Rally?

Understand some of the important things a cruising rally will do for you:

- Defining an itinerary for the most favorable conditions
- Providing support during legs with radio nets, weather predictions, and assistance from other fleet members
- Assisting you to check in and out of countries
- Providing useful local information
- Finding local interpreters for non-English-speaking countries
- Organizing preplanned tours at many destinations
- Offering valuable safety consultation
- Creating a sense of camaraderie among the fleet
- Giving an added sense of confidence to a first-time blue-water sailor

If you have limited time, a rally can help you see more of the world in a shorter period. On your own, in some countries, the check-in/check-out process may take several days, and the Panama Canal transit might introduce substantial delays.

In reviewing our logs for this book, we prepared the "Itinerary Sample" on page 135. Here you can see that we spent 159 days underway and 307 days in port. You'll need to decide for yourself if 307 days is enough for you to feel fulfilled by your world exploration or if you'll need to extend the itinerary (either inside or outside of a rally).

That said, participants need not feel obliged to follow the rally itinerary precisely. Some fleet members often left a few days before or after a scheduled departure time, and we skipped a few stops that did not interest us (and we stopped at some destinations not on the original itinerary).

You Should Probably *Not* Join a Rally If:

You have unlimited time and want to spend as much time as you like at every stop to "see the world."

You have very limited funds for boat repairs and maintenance. Getting things repaired quickly usually entails hiring local workers and paying air-freight premiums for parts, as you may not have time in a particular port to learn the ins and outs of doing the work yourself.

You want to single-hand. This entails some additional risks that rally organizers may not wish to accept.

Getting Started

The route described in this book is a complete circumnavigation, and you could theoretically start anywhere and go around.

Where should you start? That depends on where you are now. The key is to follow favorable conditions in both starting out and returning home. Here are some preferred routes:

You'll see many gorgeous sunsets on your cruise. Photo by TheConduqtor (License CC BY-SA 3.0).

From the Northeast United States

Sail to Norfolk, Virginia (or Portsmouth, Virginia). From there, sail about 1,500 nm nonstop to the Virgin Islands (either US or British, as you prefer), which entails sailing east until well clear of the Gulf Stream and then south. Then you can either join this book's route at Saint Lucia or sail direct from the Virgin Islands to Panama and join the route there (often checking into Panama in Porvenir in the San Blas Islands).

After returning to the Caribbean, you can either go back to the Northeast United States via Bermuda or sail to Florida and then coastwise back north.

From Florida and the Southeast United States

Start by sailing coastwise to southern Florida. Then sail out and enjoy the Bahamas and Turks and Caicos. Then turn south, passing east of Cuba, perhaps stopping at Jamaica, and then on to Panama.

An alternative is to sail due east from approximately Palm Beach until north of the BVIs and then turn south. The passage from the Bahamas to the Virgin Islands is directly against the trade winds and can be unpleasant if your schedule doesn't allow for significant waits for weather windows.

After returning to the Caribbean, you have an easy downwind, down-current trip back to Florida.

From the West Coast of the United States

Sail down the coast to Puerto Vallarta, Mexico, and enjoy the winter. Depart from there in February or March directly to Nuku Hiva (a passage called the "Puddle Jump").

On returning, many cruisers don't go directly up the west coast of Central America but find more favorable winds by continuing to Hawaii and then back to the West Coast.

From Europe

Sail to the Canary Islands; then sail either more or less directly to Saint Lucia or the Caribbean destination of your choice. Alternatively, sail south to the Cape Verdes and then west.

On return, one can sail north to the Cape Verdes from Saint Helena (via Ascension Island), but this route may have you arriving in Europe before spring, and many cruisers choose to continue to Saint Lucia and spend the winter in the Caribbean before returning to Europe via Bermuda.

S/V *Celebrate* Blog: Amazing Panama Canal Adventure

February 4, 2014

The adventure began with an excellent briefing pretransit, given by Paul Tetlow of the World ARC, including a canal video. (See one at worldsailing.guru/canalvideo.aspx.)

The next afternoon began with a short stay anchored in the "flats" before the start into the Gatun Locks. Our terrific Panama Canal advisors, Ricardo and Irwin, came aboard around 4:30 p.m. and we were off! They were invaluable as the leaders of our Transit Team. Our 14 boats rafted together in twos and threes to make our way through the locks. We were grateful not to be sharing a lock with a ship.

At 8:00 p.m., our great experience of seeing the line handling locks process and taping Oreo cookie packages to the lines to send them to the canal line handlers was over. Suddenly, we were done with Gatun Locks!

Now, we were so ready to anchor in Gatun Lake, get a hot dinner for the advisors and ourselves, then be ready for the advisors at 6:00 a.m. the next day.

Next: we continue our journey across Gatun Lake, passing the Centennial Bridge and a Smithsonian Nature Preserve toward the Miraflores Locks.

(To read the complete blogs, go to worldsailing.guru/blogs.)

(January 22, 2014–February 5, 2014)   *Panama Canal transit. Photo by Lyn Gateley (License CC BY 2.0).*

- Shelter Bay Marina (Cristobal/Colón)
- Panama Canal (Transit)
- La Playita Anchorage (Balboa/Flamenco)

(Reference Only—Not for Navigation)

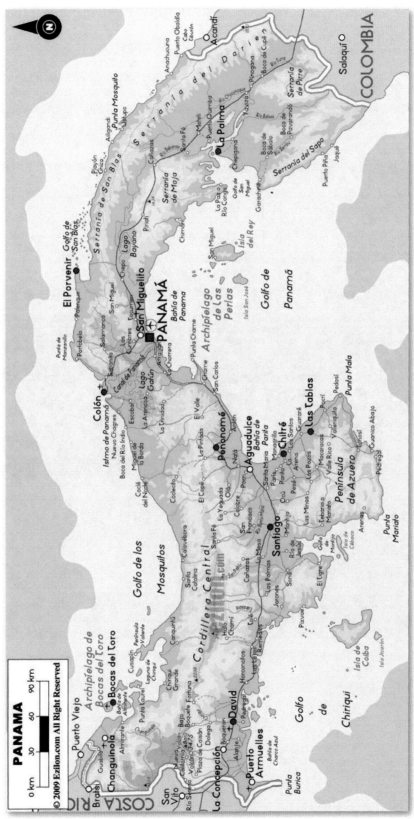

From Vidiani.com (License CC BY-SA 4.0).

QuickStart Circumnavigation Guide

PANAMA

Coordinates: 9°23' N, 79°55' W

Charts: BA 1400, BA 3111, BA 3098, BA 1401, BA 1929, BA 2258

Guides: *Panama Cruising Guide* (Bauhaus)

Ocean Passages & Landfalls (Heikell and O'Grady)

In Brief

Panama has been a strategic maritime route for over 500 years.

One of the wonders of the modern world, the Panama Canal links the Atlantic Ocean (via the Caribbean Sea) and the Pacific Ocean. But don't focus just on the canal: you'll find wonderful cruising areas in the nearby San Blas Islands on the Caribbean side and the Las Perlas Islands in the Pacific.

Websites

www.visitpanama.com

www.panamainfo.com

Customs and Immigration

US citizens need to have a passport valid for six months beyond the planned departure date, but no visa is required.

Panama Immigration office: 507-227-1448

Panama City is a modern metropolis. The mooring field of the Balboa Yacht Club is in the foreground, and La Playita is out of the frame to the right. Photo by Ekabhishek (License CC BY-SA 2.0).

■ QuickFacts

— Time: (EST) UTC-5

— Language: Spanish, English

— Currency: Officially, Panamanian balboa; in practice, US dollar

— Weather/Climate: Tropical

— Tides/Currents Caution: Tides are up to 22 feet on the Pacific side and negligible in the Caribbean. Canal currents demand caution (see "Transit Notes").

Prearrival notification is required at least forty-eight hours prior to arrival in Panama. Submit the online form here: http://www.amp.gob.pa/atraque/CaptaCartaAtraqueYates.aspx

Cruising Permits

Cruising permits are required. These are now intended to be issued for 12 months, but cruisers report that they may not extend past the expiration of the vessel registration papers. For US boats whose registration expires annually (five years in the near future), this may cause inconvenience and additional fees for renewal. Some sources say this might be avoided by using an agent to check in.

Note that this entry information is independent from the documentation needed to transit the canal, which is covered later in this chapter.

Note also that there is an exemption for vessels entering Panama to transit the canal *only*, which extends for a 72-hour stay. If you intend to do this, check with the regulatory websites and other sources for specific information.

Emergency Contacts

US Embassy: 507-207-7000

Canadian Embassy: 507-264-9731

British Embassy: 507-269-0866

1. *Shelter Bay Marina*
2. *Breakwater*
3. *Boatyard/dry storage*
4. *Entrance to Rio Chagres*

Shelter Bay Marina

(Port of Entry)

Cristobal/Colón

Coordinates: 9°22' N, 79°57' W

Charts: BA1400, BA3111, BA3098

Guides: *Panama Cruising Guide* (Bauhaus)

Ocean Passages & Landfalls (Heikell and O'Grady)

▪ QuickFacts

— Fuel: At the fuel barge in the marina, make an appointment at the marina office
— Power: 120V 60hz at marina slips
— Water: At marina slips

In Brief

The Caribbean entrance to the Panama Canal has an excellent facility at Shelter Bay Marina. This was our third visit to the marina, the first being six years earlier entering from the Pacific side.

Website

www.shelterbaymarina.com

Approach

Contact Cristobal Signal Station (port control) on VHF channel 12 (or 16) prior to entering the breakwater entrance, then follow the buoyed channel behind the breakwater, which leads to the marina entrance.

Caution: At night, buoys may not be lit.

At the Marina

What a super welcome and tie-up help from the dockmaster!

Assistance was available in the office to work with entry procedures and Panama Canal bureaucracy. They can also help arrange many repairs with the boatyard and travel lift next door.

Also, there is a small market at the marina. Finally, there is a helpful daily shuttle-bus service to Colón, which is about a half hour away, depending on the shipping in the canal.

In the evening after we arrived, we had cocktails and a good dinner on the lovely veranda at the dock marina restaurant overlooking the beautiful boats in the marina.

Shoreside Services

Supermarkets

There is a small market at the marina. In Colón, visit Rey or Super 99. Both supermarkets can be reached via the marina shuttle bus and are good for provisioning but with variable selection.

In the city of Colón, take a taxi, and do not walk around on the streets, even in the daytime. Crime is the norm.

Restaurants

We enjoyed meals on the veranda of the Shelter Bay Restaurant and Bar at the marina.

Telephones

We purchased local SIM cards in Colón and had good phone service with occasional data service. Cell phone service was available through most of the canal transit. The marina also has Wi-Fi and a pay phone.

Shopping

There is minimal shopping available in Colón. For clothing and most other purchases, a visit to Panama City is necessary (more information on page 18, in the La Playita description).

Panama has a rich history and many Spanish ruins, including this cannon emplacement at nearby Porto Bello. Celebrate *is in the distance.*

There is a large "free trade" zone in Colón that is interesting to visit, but most of the merchants are wholesale only, so call ahead if you intend to purchase something.

For your boat, there is a limited selection of parts available at the marina, but chandleries in Panama City may deliver and/or be visited via a specially arranged shuttle. You can have almost anything imported from the United States on a week's notice through Marine Warehouse, which we used. Contact: arturo@marinewarehouse.net.

Taxis

The marina will arrange a taxi if the shuttle-bus schedule doesn't fit your needs. Within Colón, taxis are available everywhere, and the taxi fare within the city is a dollar or two, so there is no reason not to take a taxi within the city.

Airport and Airlines

Tocumen International Airport is about an hour's taxi ride on the far side of Panama City (longer in rush hour). There are worldwide flights. The Crowne Plaza Hotel is at the airport for convenient overnight stays.

Accommodations

There are a few hotel rooms available at the marina that were small scaled, modern, and clean.

Howler monkeys are common in the jungles of Panama, and even if you don't see them, you'll hear them from the Shelter Bay Marina in the evenings. Photo by Jackhynes (License CC BY-SA 4.0).

Things to Do and See (Atlantic Side)

Fort San Lorenzo

Fort San Lorenzo is a ruined Spanish fortress on the promontory overlooking the mouth of the Rio Chagrés with a wonderful view. From the marina, it's about four miles through the jungle, so you may prefer to arrange a ride.

Wildlife

The marina is located on the site of an abandoned US Army training base and is surrounded by jungle. You'll find howler monkeys and tropical birds among the nearby wildlife.

Gatun Locks Visitor Center

Take the shuttle or taxi to watch ships go through the canal locks.

Smithsonian Nature Preserve

Visits can be arranged through the Gatun Locks Visitor Center. Or here:

http://www.stri.si.edu/english/visit_us/barro_colorado/index.php

Rio Chagrés

For a genuine "jungle" adventure, anchor your boat overnight in the Rio Chagrés, which is navigable to within sight of the Gatun Dam. Navigating the river mouth requires some care, but the rocks are generally made visible by the ocean swell. See *The Panama Cruising Guide* (Bauhaus).

(Reference Only—Not for Navigation)

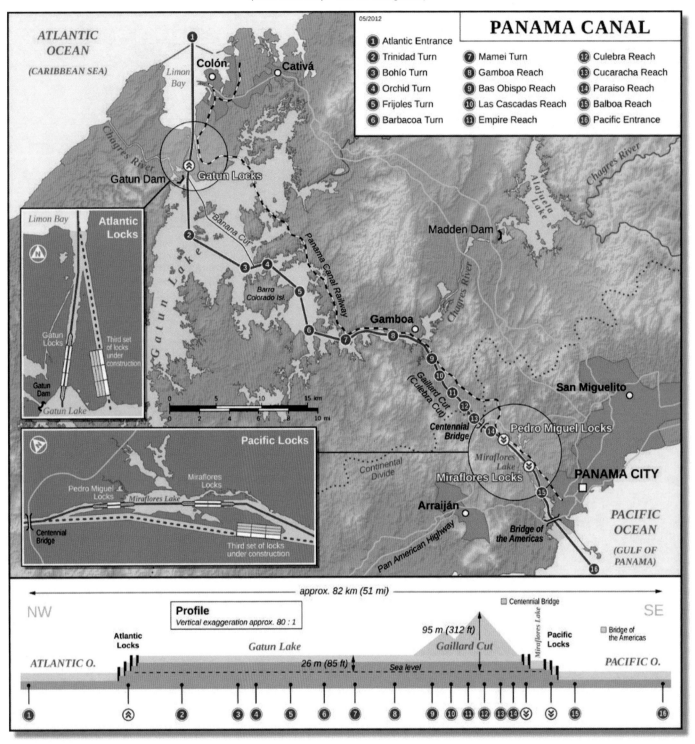

Map of the Panama Canal by Thomas Römer/OpenStreetMap data (License CC BY-SA 2.0).

　　QuickStart Circumnavigation Guide

Panama Canal Transit

Your Panama Canal transit will be one of the great memories of your sailing career. You'll get up-close-and-personal experience with the huge machinery of the locks, cruise ships, container ships, and tropical waterways and get a different perspective on the magnitude of world commerce.

We've transited the Panama Canal three times, and (also drawing on the expertise of many others) here is an overview of what you'll need to do and what you should expect. The rules and procedures do change from time to time, so no matter how well you have planned ahead, when you arrive in Panama for a transit, you'll need to check with local sources for updates to this information. The "Panama Links and Websites" sidebar on the next page is a good place to start.

Transit Background

The Panama Canal links the Caribbean Sea and the Pacific Ocean. Even though we think of the Caribbean as being east of the Pacific, looking at the map on the preceding page, you'll see that the canal runs largely northwest-southeast, and the Caribbean end of the canal is actually west of the Pacific end. Accordingly, we won't speak of "eastbound" or "westbound," because it's just too confusing; rather, we'll use "from the" Caribbean or Pacific side.

From the Caribbean, you'll enter through Limon Bay with the city of Colón and the port of Cristobal on the east side. Then you'll go up a set of three locks (Gatun Locks), which will raise your boat 85 feet to Gatun Lake, across the lake to Gaillard Cut (aka Culebra Cut), then down one lock (Pedro Miguel), then down a set of two locks (Miraflores), and finally past the La Playita Marina/Anchorage to the Gulf of Panama in the Pacific Ocean. There is a link to a flyover video via Google Earth in the "Links" sidebar to help orient you.

The route is about 45 nm long and will take one or two days, depending on the speed of your boat and the timing of your transit. If you are scheduled for an early start, you may make it in a single day. For two-day transits, you'll stay overnight at the designated anchorage in Gatun Lake. Two of the transits were completed in a single day from the Pacific side. They were long days, getting under way at 5:00 a.m. and not arriving at the destination until 9:00 p.m.

The business of the canal is to move ships from one ocean to another, but under the agreement which ceded the canal to Panama, *all* vessels must be allowed to transit. Accordingly, you can transit the canal in almost any powered craft

The tires (in garbage bags to protect your boat) and handlines you'll need for the transit.

meeting the minimum requirements. Unfortunately, although the fees may seem high to you, the economics of canal operations make yachts secondary, to be scheduled around the higher-paying ships.

All the waterways of the canal are controlled. During the approaches to the canal, you will be in radio contact with vessel traffic control—"Cristobal Signal Station" on the Cristobal/Limon side and "Flamenco Signal Station" on the Pacific side—on VHF channel 12 or channel 16. Also, you'll have an advisor from the Panama Canal Authority (ACP) on board (or a pilot if your boat measures more than 65 feet) when you are in the canal itself. You may not stop to sightsee for extra days within Gatun Lake, and you may not lower your dinghy at any time.

Preparing for Your Transit

There's considerable preparation needed for your transit. On the administrative front, you'll need to get the appropriate permits/documents and pay the fees. As a part of this process, your boat will be measured to determine the transit fees (which are based on boat length) and inspected to make sure it meets the minimum requirements. All of this can be handled through an agent, with the assistance of the marina, or you can go it alone. It can also be initiated in conjunction with the processes of checking into Panama and obtaining your cruising permit, so all the paperwork can be handled in a few taxi trips.

The best places for preparations are at Shelter Bay Marina on the Caribbean end and La Playita Marina on the Pacific end. If La Playita is unavailable, you can anchor out and dinghy into the dock at La Playita or get a mooring buoy at the Balboa Yacht Club. From the Pacific side, we moved from La Playita to BYC for a few days before our transit because they have a water-taxi service, which is preferable to a dinghy for transporting the dock lines, tires, and line handlers. On the Caribbean side, you can anchor out, but the Colón dinghy landing no longer exists, so the anchorage is less useful.

You need a minimum of four line handlers in addition to the master aboard during your transit, and you'll see why in the "During the Transit" section below. If you are using an agent, he or she can recruit line handlers for you, and they will typically be off-duty canal staff. Alternatively, you can put out a radio call on the cruisers' net and recruit other cruisers awaiting their turn to go through the canal.

TIP: We suggest you volunteer to be a line handler on another boat transiting before you take your own boat through so you can get comfortable with the process.

You will probably rent the fenders (tires in garbage bags) and the four handlines, which must be at least 125 feet long and 7/8-inch in diameter with a 1-meter eye spliced in one end. Now consider how the lines will lead on your boat. When you are in a lock with the water lowered, the lock walls will be about 40 feet above the waterline, so your lines will be leading upward from the deck cleats. As the boat is raised about 30 feet, the angle will change, and you don't want the line to foul your lifelines or damage your brightwork. If you have open chocks (as we do), you'll need to consider an alternative method of leading the lines. Fortunately, on our boat, we have snatchblocks of sufficient size, so we could lead aft lines to the primary winches.

For a quick preview of the canal transit route, watch the Google Earth video in the link to the right. Be sure to alert your friends back home so they can watch your progress through the canal on the canal webcams. And if you have an AIS transceiver on board, they can also monitor your progress on a map at the "Marine Traffic" link.

Hope she stops! We are locking down with a ship coming in astern. This view is over the dinghy mounted on our stern. Yachts are usually placed ahead of larger vessels when locking down and astern when locking up.

Minimum Requirements to Transit the Canal

- Able to maintain speed of 6 knots. (8 knots is the actual requirement, but to our knowledge this requirement has not been enforced. Slower boats may need to arrange towing.)
- Holding tank(s)
- VHF, horn, and compass
- Safe area for pilot to board
- Anchor ready to use
- Four handlines: 125 feet long, 7/8-inch diameter, 1-meter eye spliced in one end
- Fenders (tires) adequate for the rough lock walls

▪ Panama Links and Websites

- Panama Canal Transit Flyover video with Google Earth
  http://worldsailing.guru/canvideo.aspx
- Panama Canal Authority (ACP), 507-443-2293
  http://pancanal.com/
- Marine Traffic showing vessels equipped with AIS
  http://www.marinetraffic.com/en/ais/home/centerx:-80/centery:9.3/zoom:10
- Panama Canal webcams
  http://www.pancanal.com/eng/photo/camera-java.html
- Shelter Bay Marina, 507-433-3581
  http://www.shelterbaymarina.com/
- Balboa Yacht Club, 507-228-5794
  http://balboayachtclub.com.pa/
- La Playita Marina, 507-314-1730
  http://thebeachhousepanama.com/la-playita

During Your Transit

Before starting out, board your line handlers. Remember that it is your responsibility to feed them for the duration of the transit, and if you'll be staying overnight, they'll need somewhere to sleep. Wait at the designated location for your advisor. This will probably be at the anchorage F in Limon Bay on the Caribbean side or near the Balboa Yacht Club on the Pacific side. The advisor will arrive on a pilot boat that will seem like it's way too big for the job but is usually handled skillfully and will do no damage. Follow your advisor's instructions!

Buoyage is red right returning as you enter the canal from either side and reverses at Pedro Miguel Locks.

Lockage may be "center chamber," "rafted," "sidewall," or some combination, and you may not know in advance. We entered one lock anticipating center-chamber lockage and were directed to tie to a commercial tug. It is rare that a yacht gets sidewall lockage, as the lock turbulence can cause your boat to roll and your mast and/or superstructure could be damaged against the lock wall.

Occasionally, yachts will be rafted in twos or threes, in which case some of the tires and handlines will not be needed. This was arranged as part of the World ARC rally, but, in general, all yachts need to carry a full complement of tires and lines.

Your first lockage will be upward, so the lock wall will initially tower above your boat. The lock crew will toss messenger lines to your boat, each with a monkey's fist on the end (a large, ball-shaped knot). Each line handler will attach this messenger line to the appropriate handline eye, and the lock crew will pull up your handline and place its eye over a bollard at the top of the lock wall. Your line handlers will then keep tension on each of the handlines to maintain the boat in the appropriate position in the lock. If you are on a center-chamber lockage, you'll use four handlines. Rafted to another yacht, you'll need two. Rafted to a tug that is on a sidewall, you won't need to use any—you'll just be tied to the tug.

TIP: Add a package of cookies, soft drinks, or other goodies to the messenger lines to send back up to the canal line handlers—they really like it.

As water enters the lock, there will be considerable turbulence, and the boat will rise, so the line handlers need to be alert and physically capable of taking in the handline to maintain tension. If tension is not maintained, your boat may rotate and hit the lock wall, potentially causing damage.

You may also share a lock with a ship. If so, you'll usually be astern of the ship locking up and ahead of the ship locking down. *Important!* If you are behind a ship, the ship's prop wash is enormous as it gets under way. It's best to stay tied up until you know the ship's plans. There are also considerable currents to deal with. When locking down, the current will be coming from astern, making it more difficult to stop your boat when you need to.

If your transit goes for two days, your advisor will direct you to the anchorage, and he will be picked up by a pilot boat. You will need to feed and house your line handlers on board, as there is no facility for them to disembark.

After Your Transit

Before you break out the champagne and beer, make sure you are securely docked or anchored. Caution: the anchorage outside La Playita Marina, on the Pacific side, is famous for dragging anchors, partly because of the large tidal range of up to 22 feet. After leaving the Caribbean, where tides are minimal, some sailors anchor in shallow water at low tide, put out 3:1 scope on chain, and then drag free when the tide comes up.

Assuming you arrive in the evening, you'll need to get your line handlers back ashore and make arrangements to return your handlines and tires (they might be scheduled to go to another boat going the other way). After that, enjoy!

Also, be sure to send out social posts and receive the congratulations you deserve for having experienced one of the wonders of the modern world!

You'll pass under the magnificent Centennial Bridge as you approach the Pacific side. Photo by Cracker Ken (License CC BY-SA 2.0).

Image Landsat
Image © 2015 DigitalGlobe
Data SIO, NOAA, U.S. Navy, NGA, GEBCO

1. *Playita Marina*
2. *Playita/Flamenco Anchorage*
3. *Alternate anchorage for strong south winds*
4. *Flamenco Marina*
5. *Panama City*
6. *Exit from Panama Canal*
7. *Amador Causeway*

In Brief

The Pacific end of the Panama Canal is an area generally called Balboa with the Balboa Yacht Club and nearby Panama City (visible in the upper right of the image above). The Amador Causeway connects the mainland with islands that are home to the La Playita Marina, the Flamenco Marina, and anchorages. The anchorage is generally called Flamenco, but the area outside the La Playita Marina is often referred to as the La Playita Anchorage.

The Flamenco Marina is not normally open to visiting yachts, and we have never been able to reserve a slip.

You can anchor on either side of the island, depending on the wind, but the La Playita side is preferred because there is a dinghy platform at the marina.

Websites

http://thebeachhousepanama.com/la-playita/
http://balboayachtclub.com.pa

La Playita Marina/Anchorage

(Port of Entry)
Balboa/Flamenco

Coordinates: 8° 54.544' N, 79° 39.518' W
Charts: BA 1401, BA 1929, BA 3098, BA
    2258
Guides: *Panama Cruising Guide* (Bauhaus)
    Ocean Passages & Landfalls (Heikell
    and O'Grady)

- **QuickFacts**
— Fuel: At the ferry/dinghy dock
— Power: 120V 60hz at marina slips
— Water: At marina slips and ferry dock, or a water-maker can be used

Approach

As you exit the Panama Canal in Balboa, you'll be in contact with the Flamenco Signal Station on VHF channel 12 or 16. The Balboa Yacht Club (which has mooring balls) will be on the port side shortly after the Bridge of the Americas, and the La Playita entrance is about 2 nm further on. Don't cut the corner into either destination, as there are shoals.

From the Pacific, you'll see the towers of Panama City and the Bridge of the Americas, locating the entrance to the canal, on the west side of the islands.

Caution: Tides are up to 22 feet on the Pacific side. Take this into account when setting your anchor and paying out appropriate scope. Tides, coupled with the winds, currents, ocean chop, wakes from passing container ships, etc., make this an anchorage requiring some care!

At the Marina

If you don't have a slip, there is a float that serves as ferry dock, fuel dock, and dinghy dock. Caution: do not tie your dinghy to the front of the dock where the ferry lands or the back of the dock, which is high and dry at low tide.

Assistance is available to help with entry procedures and canal bureaucracy as well as many repairs.

The Flamenco Marina has a travel lift for more major repairs.

Shoreside Services

Panama City is a commercial hub to all of Latin America, and all services and shopping are available.

At the Albrook Mall, there is a small airport, where we've seen many private jets—presumably the wealthy of Latin America, who come to Panama City to shop.

Supermarkets

There is a Super 99 at Albrook Mall, about 15 minutes away by taxi or bus.

At the Multiplaza Pacific Mall, somewhat further by taxi, there is a Riba Smith, which has a greater variety and some gourmet items.

Restaurants

There are numerous restaurants within walking distance from La Playita, starting with a snack bar at the marina itself. From there, you can walk a bit further to Mi Ranchito, Hacienda Colombiana, and others on out to Bennigan's next to the Flamenco Marina.

Shopping

Albrook Mall is 15 minutes away by taxi or bus and is a huge complex with stores of every variety.

Multiplaza Pacific Mall is a very upscale mall and somewhat farther away but has designer stores.

For your boat, there is a chandlery at the marina that is a branch of the Abernathy SA marine supply. If an item is out of stock, they will often get it from their downtown store for you.

You can have almost anything imported from the United States on a week's notice through Marine Warehouse. Contact: arturo@marinewarehouse.net. Arturo's office is within walking distance.

Telephones

There is cell phone coverage in the anchorage with your Digicel or other local, prepaid SIM card.

Taxis

Taxis are the easiest way to get around and are available almost everywhere.

Airport and Airlines

Tocumen International Airport is about a 30-minute taxi ride on the far side of Panama City (longer in rush hour). There are flights worldwide, and a Crowne Plaza Hotel is on-site.

Accommodations

There is a hotel at the nearby Flamenco Marina.

Things to Do and See (Pacific Side)

Tours

Numerous interesting tours are available, including a tour we took to visit the enchanting Embera Indian Village on the Rio Chagrés River, surrounded by virgin rainforest. Several reputable tour operators can help—we used Margo Tours:
http://www.margotours.com/en/

Miraflores Locks

Go to the visitor center to learn more about the canal and the expansion project. You can also watch the shipping traffic.

Diving

Snorkeling and scuba diving trips can be arranged.

A Panama City "Party Bus"

For a popular night of fun, reserve a spot on a "party bus." It includes a bar, a live DJ on board, and room for dancing.

The Bridge of the Americas as viewed from outside the Balboa Yacht Club. Photo by Stan Shebs (License CC BY-SA 3.0).

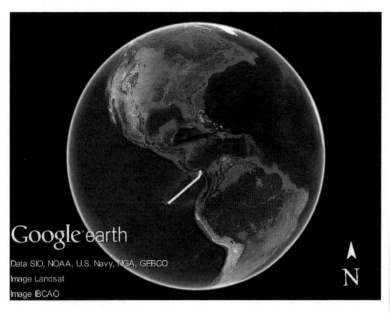

Data SIO, NOAA, U.S. Navy, NGA, GEBCO
Image Landsat
Image IBCAO

N

Passage Notes

(Panama to Galápagos)

- **QuickFacts**
  - Mileage: 788 nm
  - Duration: Seven days (including two days at Las Perlas)
  - Dates: February 5, 2014–February 12, 2014

Expected Conditions

The route typically crosses the Intertropical Convergence Zone (ITCZ, or doldrums). You can anticipate some motoring along the way.

Initially, "it was some of the most perfect sailing we had ever seen," Captain Charlie said. There were big moon nights and sunny days. We saw dolphins, sailfish, and flying fish and had tiny squid on the deck.

Crossing the equator was such a life highlight, we celebrated with a bottle of champagne.

Crossing the equator is cause for celebration aboard Celebrate! *(Champagne compliments of Jay and Laurie Ailworth.)*

Places We Visited along the Way

Las Perlas Islands

We anchored at Contadora Island at the beautiful beach in front of the Villa Hotel Romantica. The restaurant and bar views were stunning. The islands also offer an extensive cruising grounds.

We anchored at 8°37.162' N, 79°02.112' W.

Other Possible Stops

- Mainland Ecuador
- Pitcairne Island
- Easter Island
- Gambier Islands

The picturesque beach at the anchorage on Isla Contadora in the Las Perlas group. Photo by Katarzyna Sierocińska (License Free Art).

Arrival

We passed Kicker Rock on February 12, 2014, just as it was getting light. Gorgeous Galápagos at last!

S/V *Celebrate* Blog: Spectacular Sharks at Kicker Rock, Giant Tortoises, a Volcano, and a Grand Treehouse!

February 16, 2014

What an experience! After a great boat ride to the gap of famous Kicker Rock, we were up close and personal snorkeling with groups of sharks and eagle rays. A nice lunch was served, and then we were off to a close-by beach for swimming and bird watching. What fun!

We took the best taxi tour of our lives with Carlos the previous day to see a preserve of giant tortoises (they are big!), visited a volcano that now holds drinking water for the community of 8,000 people, and saw a very grand treehouse in an ancient cottonwood tree. Entering the treehouse is very exciting on a wooden stick bridge high in the air. I have the photos to prove it!

(To read the complete blogs, go to worldsailing.guru/blogs.)

GALÁPAGOS

(February 12, 2014–March 4, 2014)   *Galápagos tortoise. Photo by Daniel Ramirez (License CC BY 2.0).*

- Wreck Bay Anchorage (Bahia de Naufragio, Puerto Moreno, Isla San Cristobal)
- Academy Bay Anchorage (Bahia Academia, Puerto Ayora, Isla Santa Cruz)

(Reference Only—Not for Navigation)

Map by Galápagos_Islands_topographic_map-de.svg: Eric Gaba (Sting - fr:Sting), translated by NordNordWest derivative work: MatthewStevens (Galápagos_Islands_topographic_map-de.svg). (License CC BY-SA 3.0.)

GALÁPAGOS ISLANDS (ECUADOR)

Coordinates: 00°53' S, 89°36' W

Charts: BA1375

Guides: *Ocean Passages & Landfalls* (Heikell and O'Grady)
South Pacific Anchorages (Clay)
Pacific Crossing Guide (RCC)

In Brief

Located in the South Pacific Ocean, the volcanic islands are a part of the South American country of Ecuador—about 600 nm offshore.

The Galápagos Islands are noted for their unique wildlife and for having been visited by Charles Darwin during his voyage on the sailing vessel *Beagle*.

There are many restrictions on visiting yachts, and you are not free to anchor, explore, or dive wherever you wish. Outside of the anchorages on the following pages, you must contract an onboard national park guide to accompany you.

Websites

www.Galápagostourist.org
www.ecuadortouristboard.com

■ QuickFacts

— Time: (EST) UTC-9
— Language: Spanish
— Currency: US dollar
— Weather/Climate: Subtropical
— Tides/Currents: Insignificant

Customs and Immigration

It is recommended that you use an agent for entry. We used Ricardo Arenas at www.sailinggalapagos.com.ec.

Wreck Bay and Academy Bay are the ports of entry normally used.

Magestic Kicker Rock is one of your first sights on approaching Isla San Cristobal. After checking in, a snorkeling tour here is one of the top attractions.

The marine iguana is one of many novel creatures you'll encounter in the Galápagos. These would sometimes swim past our boat while we were at anchor. Photo by Maurizio Costanzo (License CC BY 2.0).

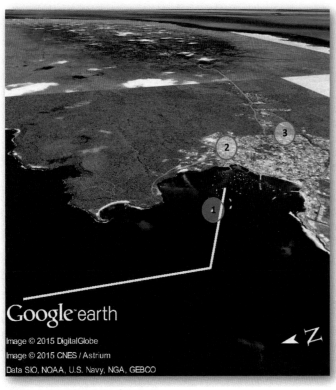

1. Wreck Bay Anchorage
2. Water taxi dock
3. Town of Puerto Moreno

Wreck Bay Anchorage

(Port of Entry)
Bahia de Naufragio, Puerto Moreno, Isla San Cristobal

Coordinates: 00°44' N, 89°36' W

Charts: BA1375

Guides: *Ocean Passages & Landfalls*
(Heikell and O'Grady)
South Pacific Anchorages (Clay)
Pacific Crossing Guide (RCC)

▪ QuickFacts
— Fuel: Jerry cans from the gas station in town
— Power: None
— Water: Jerry cans from ashore, but water in the anchorage is clean enough for watermaker use

In Brief

The sound of barking sea lions filled our ears at pretty Puerto Moreno, located at the northwest coast of Isla San Cristobal. While there are wonderful tours here, shopping, provisioning, and boat services are better at Isla Santa Cruz.

Websites

www.Galápagostourist.org

Approach

It's a straightforward entry with a buoyed entrance, but the anchorage is best entered during daylight, as it is crowded with local craft. Our agent, Ricardo Arenas, met us on our boat with a host of government officials to clear us in.

At the Anchorage

The designated area for yachts is the east side of the bay. There is reasonable holding and shelter. Also, there is a good water-taxi service but limited space at the town dock at the head of the bay.

At the end of the day, with the twinkle of anchor lights and the glow of shore lights, it looks like a fairyland.

Sea lions are plentiful, and this pup greeted us at the beach on one of our island tours. They're also a treat to watch when diving or snorkeling.

Shoreside Services

Market

The Mercado Municipal is opposite the port captain's office. When we visited, the selection was very limited.

Restaurants

A short walk from the landing dock, the charming Miconia open-air restaurant is above the Miconia Hotel lobby and comes complete with a beautiful bay view. At dinner our first night, after two Cuba librés and an outstanding dinner of mixed seafood barbeque on our table grill, we really felt happy.

Telephones
We had no cell phone service.

Shopping
There is a variety of tourist shops along the waterfront, but we found the shopping to be much more varied and interesting at our next stop at Isla Santa Cruz.

Airport and Airlines
The small airport is a short ride from town and is serviced by both interisland and direct flights to the mainland (Ecuador).

Water Taxis
There is a good water-taxi service on VHF channel 14. These are needed to ferry you to and from shore, as there is no dock where you can leave a dinghy while you go ashore.

Taxis
Taxis are usually extended-cab 4x4s and are available in town. They are happy to take you on island tours. (We used Carlos.)

Accommodations
Rooms are available at the Hotel Miconia.

Things to Do and See

Kicker Rock
Kicker Rock is the famous split rock you see as you near the Galápagos island of San Cristobal. Also, you can take an excellent snorkeling tour there with sharks and eagle rays.

Tour around the Island
We took a fantastic tour around the island with Carlos. First, we visited a grand treehouse in an ancient cottonwood tree; the entrance is very exciting on a wooden stick bridge high in the air.

Next, we visited the volcano, which is shrouded in mist much of the time. It's interesting to note that, as Isla San Cristobal is one of the older Galápagos islands, its volcanic crater is much more vegetated than its barren younger cousins.

The last taxi-tour stop was the giant tortoise preserve. The tortoises are big! There is also a tortoise nursery to bring back the population of giant tortoises.

The frigate bird on Galápagos inflates a scarlet throat pouch and has a unique angular appearance in flight with its forked tail. Photos (left) by Paul Krawczuk and (right) by Sophie Robson (both License CC BY 2.0).

The blue-footed booby is another wonderful sight in the Galápagos. Photo by DickDanlies (http://carolinabirds.org) (License CC BY-SA 3.0).

1. *Academy Bay Anchorage*
2. *Water taxi dock*
3. *Town of Puerto Ayora*

Academy Bay Anchorage

(Port of Entry)
Bahia Academia, Puerto Ayora, Isla Santa Cruz

Coordinates: 00°44.908' N, 90°18.607' W
Charts: BA1375
Guides: *Ocean Passages & Landfalls*
(Heikell and O'Grady)

- **QuickFacts**
  — Fuel: Jerry cans from the nearby gas station. Also, enterprising panga drivers with large containers and a pump may deliver fuel to your boat. Be careful to check the quantities
  — Power: None
  — Water: Jerry cans from shore; also, the anchorage is clean for watermaker use

In Brief

Puerto Ayora is a colorful port city with the Charles Darwin Research Station nearby. There are pelicans galore, and the occasional swimming marine iguana going past your boat.

This is the commercial center of the Galápagos Islands and the principal entry point for tourists arriving by air. Santa Cruz Island runs the gamut from dry vegetation in the low areas to the lush tropical trees of the "highlands," just minutes away by car.

Websites

www.Galápagostourist.org

Approach

Make your approach in daylight. You will have to skirt around the shallows on the north side of the anchorage and circle other boats to find a spot. Don't rely on your GPS; our anchor position showed us firmly on land on the chart plotter.

At the Anchorage

This is a crowded anchorage, and we used a stern anchor to limit swinging. Dinghy landing is not allowed, but the water-taxi service is available on VHF channel 14.

The anchorage at Puerto Ayora is crowded with commercial craft and yachts. Stern anchors keep boats from swinging into each other. Photo by A Flores López (License CC BY-SA 3.0).

Shoreside Services

The town of Puerto Ayora is the center of the Galápagos Islands, and all services are available with varying degrees of convenience.

Market

The mercado (about a 10-minute walk from the dock) has a range of fresh fruit and produce, some locally grown and some from the mainland.

Supermarkets

There is a nice market at the town dock with packaged foods, water, liquor, and a fresh bakery (great bread!). Further up the main street, on the right side, there are several smaller stores.

Restaurants

Many wonderful restaurants are just a few minutes' walk from the dock. Some examples:

The Rock Café is upscale, with reasonable prices, and a popular spot.

Il Giardino has great Italian food in an attractive two-story open-air restaurant and has super ice cream!

Hotel Sol y Mar's upscale restaurant has a spectacular flaming sushi dragon roll.

Telephones

We had no cell phone service. We could Skype from the Wi-Fi ashore and reach many local services by VHF.

Shopping

For the boat, there is a chandlery in town that can also import parts if you are staying long enough. Otherwise, shipping in parts (which all go through mainland Ecuador) can be a lengthy process. Also, there is a machine shop within walking distance that can fabricate most of the parts you may need.

In general, there are many tourist shops that sell a variety of merchandise.

Water Taxis

There is a good water-taxi service, which you call on VHF channel 14. This is needed to ferry you to and from shore, as there is no dinghy dock.

Taxis

Taxis are plentiful and cheap in town and will take you touring if you want.

Airport and Airlines

Seymour/Baltra Airport is on an island just north of Santa Cruz. The taxi ride is about a half hour to the ferry dock and a five-minute ferry ride, followed by a fifteen-minute bus ride, which takes you to the airport.

Air service can take you to other islands as well as the Ecuador mainland.

Accommodations

There are many hotels in town. A *National Geographic* group was staying at the Red Mangrove.

Things to Do and See

Tours

Wildlife, historical, and archeological areas abound, and there are many tour companies. We found a knowledgeable taxi driver to take us to the highlands to visit beautiful craters, tortoises, and lava tubes.

Diving

Galápagos Islands diving is world class, and there are about 30 dive sites around Isla Santa Cruz. There are, however, restrictions, and you must dive with a local dive master (not off your own boat).

The Galápagos are located at the confluence of equatorial and Antarctic currents, causing an abundance and variety of sea life that are unparalleled.

There are several reputable dive shops in town. On my dives, the dive master had a camera and distributed wonderful underwater pictures and videos after the dive. The scuba trip to Gordon Rocks was spectacular, with the rocks rising directly from about 100 feet for a wall dive. Also, there was a school of hammerhead sharks and a very up-close view of a huge sea turtle. The dive was topped off with a school of rays and an enormous variety of reef fish.

Scuba diving is one of the great attractions of Galápagos. With the meeting of tropical and Antarctic currents, there is a variety of sea life unrivalled in my diving experience around the world. That's me on the left.

N

Passage Notes
(Galápagos to Hiva Oa)

- **QuickFacts**
  — Mileage: 3,352 nm
  — Duration: 22 days
  — Dates: March 4, 2014–March 26, 2014

Expected Conditions

At over 3,000 nm, this is the longest passage on a world circumnavigation.

You may have to go somewhat south of the Galápagos to pick up the trade winds, but then you should have a great downwind run to the Marquesas in French Polynesia.

There may be squalls and some variability. We had generally wonderful weather but encountered light winds 500 miles out from Hiva Oa and motored in.

Also, we saw whopping whales' tails from a pod a few feet from our bow and dolphins with their babies jumping all around the boat. Plus, there were flying fish flopping into our laps in the cockpit at night.

Places We Visited along the Way

None, we went straight to the Marquesas in French Polynesia.

Other Possible Stops

- Isla Isabela is the easternmost of the Galápagos anchorages. Geologically, it is among the newest islands and is much more desolate.
- Further afield, Pitcairn Island, the Easter Islands, and the Gambier Islands are all possible to visit but are more off the beaten cruiser route.

Arrival

We arrived in French Polynesia as Captain Cook did—by sail. The anchorage at Hiva Oa can be crowded, so a daylight arrival is recommended. We arrived on March 26, 2014.

Dolphins may be your only visitors for 3,000 miles. When they play in your bow wave, it is a completely joyous sight. We saw a single freighter (at a great distance) and two other cruisers during the entire passage. Photo by NASA.

S/V *Celebrate* Blog: Land Ho! The Marquesas!

March 28, 2014

After 3,000 nm plus from the Galápagos, we have arrived at the Marquesas in French Polynesia as Captain Cook did, by sailboat. Our port of entry is the island of Hiva Oa, where the famous painter Paul Gauguin is buried just above our anchorage in the village of Atuona.

(To read the complete blogs, go to worldsailing.guru/blogs)

FRENCH POLYNESIA

(March 26, 2014–May 11, 2014)

Polynesian dancers. Photo courtesy Tahiti Tourisme.

- Taaoa Bay Anchorage (Atuona, Hiva Oa, Marquesas)
- Taiohae Bay Anchorage (Nuku Hiva, Marquesas)
- Marina Taina (Papeete, Tahiti, Society Islands)
- Maikai Marina/Moorage (Vaitre, Bora Bora, Society Islands)

(Reference Only—Not for Navigation)

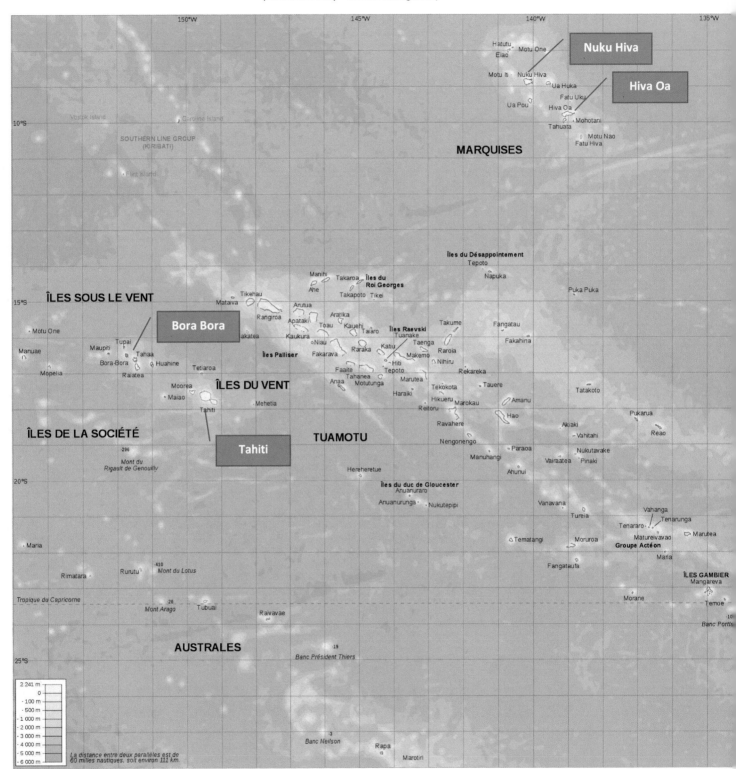

From Vidiani.com (License CC BY-SA 4.0).

FRENCH POLYNESIA

Coordinates: 09°48' S, 139°00' W

Charts: BA 1382, BA 998, BA 1060, BA 1107

Guides: *Ocean Passages & Landfalls* (Heikell and O'Grady)

South Pacific Anchorages (Clay)

Pacific Crossing Guide (RCC)

Landfalls of Paradise (Hinz)

Charlie's Charts of Polynesia (Wood)

Yachtsmen's Guide to French Polynesia (Government of French Polynesia)

In Brief

Located in the South Pacific Ocean and spread out over 1,200 miles, French Polynesia is a South Seas paradise. It's divided into five island groups, of which three are commonly visited by yachts: the Marquesas Group, the Tuomotus, and the Society Islands.

The "Coconut Milk Run" is a well-used route in the South Pacific. It starts in the Marquesas and passes through French Polynesia then on to the Cook Islands, Fiji, Vanuatu, and Australia. Also, there are many variations—for instance, leaving from Tonga or Fiji for New Zealand. We mostly followed the more direct route and did not turn off for New Zealand, as our time was limited.

Caution: All buoyage is IALA System A with green to starboard and red to port when entering a port, the reverse of the United States.

Navigation throughout French Polynesia is generally

French Polynesia is famous for black pearls. You can visit farms in the Tuomotus. Photo by Liz Saldaña (License CC BY-SA 2.0).

straightforward, with well-marked (or obvious) channel entrances.

▪ QuickFacts

— Time: UTC -9:30 (Marquesas) to UTC -10:00 (Tahiti, Bora Bora)
— Language: French
— Currency: CFP
— Weather/Climate: Tropical year-round
— Tides/Currents: Insignificant (Caution: strong currents at narrow entrances to some atoll lagoons)

Websites

Each port location mentioned has its own website listed on that port page.

Customs and Immigration

It can be practical to use an agent for entry. We used Laurent of Polynesia Yacht Services.

Entry formalities in the Marquesas are handled at the police stations in Hiva Oa and Nuku Hiva, where we visited.

A bond is required to guarantee your subsequent departure from French Polynesia, but it might be waived if using an agent.

Visa

Citizens of the United States can stay for up to 30 days without a visa.

TIP: There is a free guide, "Yachtsmen's Guide to French Polynesia," which is produced annually by the Port Authority. It often has current useful information. Ask for it at your port of entry.

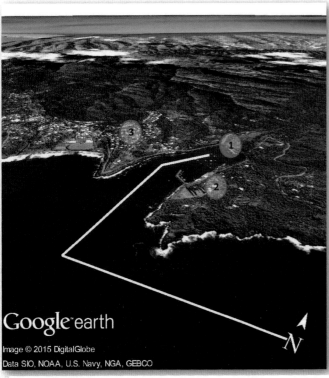

Image © 2015 DigitalGlobe
Data SIO, NOAA, U.S. Navy, NGA, GEBCO

1. Anchorage
2. Dinghy landing
3. Town of Atuona

Taaoa Bay Anchorage

(Port of Entry)

Atuona, Hiva Oa, Marquesas

Coordinates: 09°48.185' S, 139°01.072' W (our actual anchorage position)

Charts: BA4607, BA 1649

Guides: *Ocean Passages & Landfalls* (Heikell and O'Grady)

South Pacific Anchorages (Clay)

Pacific Crossing Guide (RCC)

Landfalls of Paradise (Hinz)

Charlie's Charts of Polynesia (Wood)

Yachtsmen's Guide to French Polynesia (Government of French Polynesia)

In Brief

Taaoa Bay Anchorage at Atuona is located on the south side of Hiva Oa Island, and the village has some services.

Hiva Oa is the nearest port of entry to the Galápagos Islands. For voyagers arriving from Mexico, Nuku Hiva is closer and has more services.

Website

www.marquises-hivaoa.org.pf

Approach

Make the approach by day so there is no difficulty in finding the anchorage in the northern corner of the bay.

At the Anchorage

There is reasonable holding and shelter. A stern anchor is recommended to limit swinging and keep the bow pointing toward any swell that may enter the bay. There is a pier on the east side of the bay that is used by the supply ship, but you can stern tie to it after checking that no ship is due in.

The dinghy landing is rough concrete and can be difficult if there is a swell.

▪ QuickFacts

— Fuel: Jerry cans from the gas station next to the dinghy dock
— Power: None
— Water: None potable

Shoreside Services

Market

The gas station next to the dinghy dock has a small store with fresh bread daily.

Restaurant

There is a café in town.

Telephones

There is a pay phone outside the post office.

Shopping

There are small-island type shops in town, which is a short taxi ride or a healthy walk from the dinghy dock.

Taxis

Taxis are casual, meaning there were a few people with vehicles who would take you places for a charge but not a formal taxi service.

Airport and Airlines

The small airport is a short taxi ride from the anchorage with interisland service to Tahiti by Air Tahiti.

Accommodations

A few bed and breakfasts.

Things to Do and See

The Hiva Oa tourist office has part-time support just above the dinghy dock.

Visit the Paul Gauguin Museum in town and continue to the Jacques Brel Museum.

Visit the burial places of Paul Gauguin and Belgian singer/songwriter Jacques Brel at the Calvary Cemetery.

These stone tikis are common on Hiva Oa. Photo by Amrican at de.wikipedia (License CC BY-SA 3.0).

Hiva Oa from the south. The anchorage is just to the right of center. Photo by Hervé (License CC BY-SA 3.0).

Passage Notes
(Hiva Oa to Nuku Hiva)

Expected Conditions

We experienced light winds of 10 knots with clear weather and 0.5 knots of current with us on a beautiful overnight passage.

Places We Visited along the Way

Hanamoenoa Bay (09°54.242′ S, 139°06.311′ W—our anchorage position) is noted as the most beautiful anchorage in the Marquesas, and we agree! An exquisite beach with a lush tropical island view. It was paradise found!

"My trip up the mast to recover a halyard gave a spectacular vista, with two giant rays gliding through the crystal-clear water."

Captain Charlie

Other Possible Stops

Hakaahau on Ua Pou. Also a port of entry located between Hiva Oa and Nuku Hiva.

Arrival in Nuku Hiva

As from the pages of Herman Melville's *Typee*, we heard the nighttime drumbeats on our arrival April 1, 2014.

▪ QuickFacts
— Time: UTC 9:30
— Mileage: 84 nm
— Duration: Four days (including two days at Hanamoenoa Bay)
— Dates: March 28, 2014–April 1, 2014

Manta rays are among the spectacular sights. Photo by Stevenson_john (License CC BY-SA 3.0).

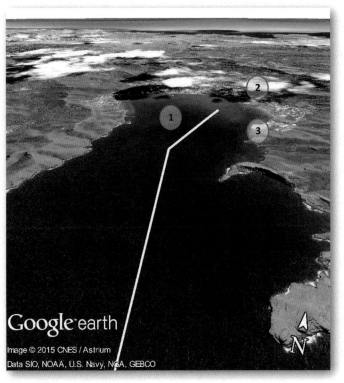

1. Anchorage
2. Dinghy landing
3. Ship quay/fuel station

Taiohae Bay Anchorage

(Port of Entry)

Nuku Hiva, Marquesas

Coordinates: 08°55.088' S, 140°5.795' W
(our actual anchorage position)

Charts: BA4607, BA 1649

Guides: *Ocean Passages & Landfalls* (Heikell
and O'Grady)

South Pacific Anchorages (Clay)

Pacific Crossing Guide (RCC)

Landfalls of Paradise (Hinz)

Charlie's Charts of Polynesia (Wood)

Yachtsmen's Guide to French Polynesia
(Government of French Polynesia)

- ▪ **QuickFacts**
- — Time: UTC 9:30
- — Fuel: There is a gas station with a very long hose that can reach the ship dock, where you can stern tie to fuel if the swell is low.
- — Power: None
- — Water: Reported unpotable, but water in the anchorage is clean enough for watermaker use

In Brief

Nuku Hiva is the nearest French Polynesian island to Mexico and the Pacific Coast of the United States. It is the common landfall for voyagers arriving from Mexico.

Websites

None available at the time of writing.

Approach

Entering the bay is straightforward, with no difficulty in finding the anchorage, which is located on the south side of Nuku Hiva Island.

At the Anchorage

The anchorage has plenty of space and offers good protection, although there can be considerable swell.

The dinghy landing is behind the breakwater and has ladders. When a swell is running in the bay, the dinghy landing area, particularly down the northern side, will have lots of motion.

There are some shops and services in the village.

Shoreside Services

Market

Two minimart-sized grocery stores are within walking distance of the dinghy landing.

Restaurants

There is an open-air café on the dock, and there are several restaurants in the village.

Shopping

A few tourist shops are near the dock.

For the boat: Nuku Hiva Yacht Services was very helpful in getting temporary replacement batteries from the gas station and installing them so we could continue on our way.

Telephones

There is a pay phone outside the post office. Our cell phone worked in the anchorage.

Taxis

Taxis are casual, but rides may be arranged with locals.

Airport and Airlines

The small airport is on the north side of the island with interisland flights.

Accommodations

A few boutique hotels exist.

Things to Do and See

Take a walk into town, and visit the shops along the way.

See a dance demonstration.

Tour the island by taxi.

Relax.

The wide-open anchorage at Nuku Hiva with the village spread out along the shore. Photo by Sémhur (License CC BY-SA 3.0).

Passage Notes
(Nuku Hiva to Papeete, Tahiti)

Expected Conditions

We had outstanding downwind sailing for four days.

Caution: This route passes through the Tuamotus. Whether you are passing through or planning to stop, be aware that the islands are largely unlit and are so low in the water that they are mostly not visible from any distance away. In our experience, the electronic charts were sufficiently accurate to avoid the islands. Keep a good lookout.

Places We Visited along the Way

None; our new house batteries awaited us in Papeete, Tahiti. We could have had the batteries sent to Nuku Hiva by ship, but this would have taken four weeks. It was easier just to proceed to Tahiti, where they were in stock.

Other Possible Stops

The Tuamotu Archipelago has excellent diving and pearl farms.

Arrival

Our Tahiti landfall was on April 8, 2014. We sailed to a beautiful, lush, mountainous terrain. It was a perfect place to call home for the next three weeks.

■ **QuickFacts**
— Mileage: 759 nm
— Duration: Five days
— Dates: April 3, 2014–April 8, 2014

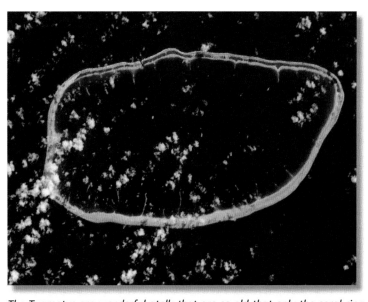

The Tuamotus are wonderful atolls that are so old that only the coral ring remains after the central volcanic peak has eroded away. Compare with the much newer Marquesas, which are volcanic without surrounding coral reefs. Note the tiny break in the reef, which offers entrance to the lagoon. Even with the small tidal range of the central Pacific, large currents will flow through the opening. Photo by NASA.

1. *Entry through well-marked break in reef*
2. *Marina Taiae*

Marina Taina

(Port of Entry)
Papeete, Tahiti, Society Is-
lands

Coordinates: 17°35' S, 149°36' W

Charts: BA 1382, BA 998

Guides: *Ocean Passages & Landfalls* (Heikell
and O'Grady)
South Pacific Anchorages (Clay)
Pacific Crossing Guide (RCC)
Landfalls of Paradise (Hinz)
Charlie's Charts of Polynesia
(Wood)
Yachtsmen's Guide to French Poly-
nesia (Government of French Poly-
nesia)

▪ QuickFacts

— Time: UTC-10
— Fuel: Fuel dock at the marina
— Power: 220v 50Hz
— Water: Potable water at the dock

In Brief

Located on the northwest side of the island of Tahiti, Papeete is the capital of French Polynesia. It is also the center of amazing French food and wine.

The Papeete harbor is closer to downtown but was under construction when we visited.

Website

tahiti-tourisme.com

Approach

Marina Taina is on the west side of the island. Round the northwest corner of the island with a wide berth. The surrounding reef is well marked but projects much farther from the island than one might expect. Then enter from the west through a marked break in the surrounding reef about a mile south of the marina. The entrance can be rough in a southwest swell but is generally safe.

Alternatively, enter through the main Papeete harbor entrance, then work your way around the island. Contact Harbor Control on VHF channel 12 before entering or leaving Papeete harbor.

At the Marina

Most dockage is Mediterranean-style mooring with lazyline pickup with help from the marina dinghy. The marina diver helps to secure the lazy lines and both sides. When the swell is from the southwest, it can come in over the reef and cause considerable boat motion. Don't snug up too close to the seawall.

There are also a few side-tie docks, and the marina has good services. It is about 15 minutes by taxi from downtown Papeete.

Most of the mooring buoys are taken by local vessels, but you can call the marina and inquire if one is available.

Shoreside Services

Papeete is a major metropolis with all the services you might expect.

Markets

As this is the center of French Polynesia, the food shopping is outstanding.

For the "island" market experience, go to the downtown marketplace. It's a full block of local vendors selling local and imported food, including interesting ready-to-eat items.

Supermarkets

Adjacent to the marina there is a smaller supermarket (just past the McDonald's) that has everything you need. The market would be considered excellent if it weren't for the massive Cara Fours somewhat further away.

The Cara Fours supermarket is a 15-minute walk in the other direction and is an experience not to be missed. It is the largest gourmet grocery store we've seen.

Restaurants

Many wonderful restaurants abound. The nearest are the Italian restaurant in the marina and the upscale Pink Coconut at the south end of the marina.

Shopping

For your boat: There is a chandlery at the marina and another downtown, along with excellent hardware stores.

Tahiti is famous for its black Tahitian pearls. You can get them in town if you missed the chance to stop at one of the pearl farms in the Tuamotus on the way to Tahiti.

Every variety of clothing is available downtown.

Telephones

You'll want to purchase a local SIM card.

Taxis

Taxis are plentiful.

Airport and Airlines

Fa'a'ā International Airport is about halfway between the marina and downtown Papeete. As Tahiti is a major tourist hub, from here you can get direct flights worldwide.

Accommodations

There are numerous hotels around Tahiti, from grand to economy.

A view of Tahiti with Marina Taina in the foreground. Photo by Remi Jouan (License CC BY-SA 2.5).

Things to Do and See

Tours
A circle-island bus tour is a good way to get an overview of the island and its history while viewing the beautiful botanical gardens, cascading waterfalls, ancient worship sites, and the Tahiti Museum.

Diving
Tahiti has excellent reef and wall dives with great sights of white-tipped reef sharks.

Dinner Shows
The Intercontinental Hotel has a wonderful dinner show with Tahitian dancers.

Numerous sharks inhabit the reefs surrounding Tahiti. Photo by Manoel Lemos (License CC BY-SA 2.0).

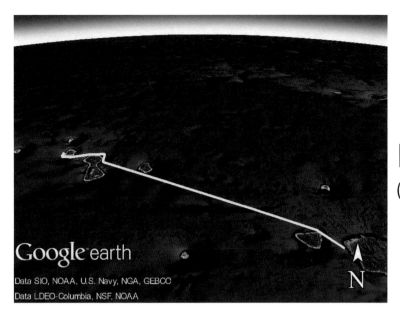

Passage Notes
(Papeete to Bora Bora)

Expected Conditions

This is mostly nice sailing but with some squalls.

Places We Visited along the Way

Moorea

(17°30.244' S, 149°49.195' W—our anchor position.) We anchored at Cook's Bay for several lazy days. There is a cute hotel called Bali with a restaurant and dinghy dock. It is very boat friendly.

Raiatea

(16°49.083' S, 151°24.965' W—our anchor position.) We passed easily through the two islets at the entry of Passe Iriru into Baie Faaroa to anchor at one of the most serene places we have ever been.

■ **QuickFacts**
— Mileage: 167 nm
— Duration: Eight days, including seven days in Moorea and Raiatea
— Dates: April 26, 2014–May 4, 2014

Other Possible Stops

Huahine and Tahaa, with many possible anchorages.

Arrival

We made landfall at beautiful Bora Bora on May 4, 2014, catching a mooring ball at MaiKai Marina.

Spectacular, lush Moorea is definitely worth the visit. It has beautiful anchorages, and it's only a short ferry ride to/from Tahiti. Photo by Michael R Perry (License CC BY 2.0).

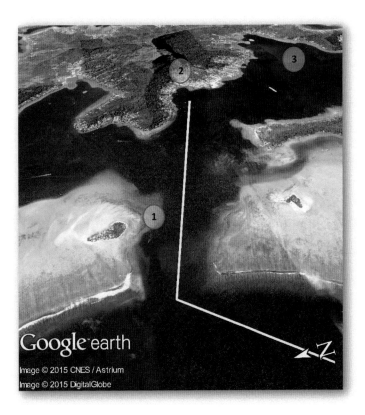

1. Entry through well-marked break in reef
2. MaiKai Marina
3. Bloody Mary's Restaurant

MaiKai Marina/Moorage

(Port of Entry)
Vaitape, Bora Bora, Society Islands

Coordinates: 16°30' N, 151°45' W

Charts: BA 1060, BA 1107

Guides: *Ocean Passages & Landfalls* (Heikell and O'Grady)
South Pacific Anchorages (Clay)
Pacific Crossing Guide (RCC)
Landfalls of Paradise (Hinz)
Charlie's Charts of Polynesia (Wood)
Yachtsmen's Guide to French Polynesia (Government of French Polynesia)

▪ QuickFacts

— Time: UTC-10
— Fuel: Fuel dock is just south of the marina
— Power: 220v 50hz (at docks)
— Water: On the dock, and water in the mooring field is clean enough for watermaker use

MaiKai has an excellent dinghy dock if you are on a mooring ball or anchored out.

There are beautiful lights at night in the marina swimming pool.

Shoreside Services

Supermarket

There are two supermarkets in town that are well stocked but small relative to the shopping in Tahiti.

Restaurants

Try the gourmet restaurant at the MaiKai Marina.

In Brief

Those in the know claim that Bora Bora is the most beautiful island in the Pacific.

Website

www.maikaimarina.com

Approach

The only entrance through the surrounding reef is on the west side of the island. Well charted, the pass through the reef is broad and clear with port and starboard beacons. Keep going on the entry bearing, and you will arrive at the MaiKai Marina and mooring field.

At the Marina/Moorings

There are a few stern-to spaces at the dock, and about 20 mooring balls are available. Anchoring nearby is not practical, as the water is quite deep, but it is possible further south in the bay.

There are also several nice restaurants as you walk into town.

Bloody Mary's Restaurant and Bar is a fun trip in a fast dinghy, about five miles south, with a convenient dock. The bar has unique tree-stump stools and sawdust floors with great cocktails. You can also anchor out in the lagoon nearby.

Shopping

The town near the marina offers various tourist shops, including pearl jewelry within walking distance.

Telephones

We had cell phone service with our Tahiti SIM card.

Taxis

Taxis can usually be found at the main dock in town, which is about a 10-minute walk.

Airport and Airlines

The small airport on the outlying reef is accessible by ferry or motor launch. There is regular service to Tahiti with several flights daily on Air Tahiti.

Accommodations

You can choose from many tourist resorts with several on the outlying reefs having cottages on stilts over the water.

The Four Seasons resort in Bora Bora with cottages over the lagoon. Photo by Didierlefort (License CC BY-SA 3.0).

Things to Do and See

Tours

Visit the tourist office at the main ferry dock in town.

Take a round-island tour in an open-air Jeep 4x4 that offers incredible views as well as interesting fortifications from World War II. We used Vavau Adventures tours with "George of the Jungle" as our guide. The trip included samples of papaya and breadfruit along with demonstrations of tie-dye cloth dying. Several ultrasteep roads took us up Mount Pahia for incredible views. Also, we visited Fitiiu Point to see historical World War II artillery along with ancient worship sites.

Diving

Bora Bora has excellent diving through several dive shops, and snorkel trips are also available.

The dive shop we used was Top Dives, right at the MaiKai Marina. On the scuba trip, there were giant sea cucumbers, brilliant blue giant clams, and colorful sea anemones with bright red undersides.

Giant clams are one of the wonderful diving experiences of the lagoon at Bora Bora. Photo by Derek Keats (License CC BY 2.0).

Passage Notes

(French Polynesia/Bora Bora to Niue)

Expected Conditions

We had wonderful trade wind sailing with a few squalls.

We were having such fun sailing and surfing down the swells! At the end, we had to slow our speed to arrive in the daytime.

Also, at one point the waves beside the boat erupted with jumping dolphins only a few feet on each side of the boat.

Places We Visited along the Way

None. We started out with a planned visit to Suwarrow, but the predicted weather would have made passage on to the island of Niue dead upwind, so we cut the corner and went directly to Niue.

Other Possible Stops

Suwarrow (with several alternate spellings)—an uninhabited atoll that is a popular stop when the wind is right.

Arrival

The Niue Yacht Club maintains a mooring field, as the anchorage is not practical. We arrived on May 20, 2014.

- ■ QuickFacts
  - — Mileage: 1,325 nm
  - — Duration: Nine days
  - — Dates: May 11, 2014–May 20, 2014

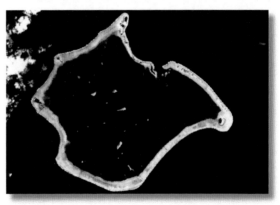

Suwarrow is another ancient atoll with no central volcano. It is uninhabited, but there is a ranger there seasonally. Photo by NASA.

S/V *Celebrate* Blog: High Commissioner Party and Rally Dinner with Dancers and Singers in Niue!

May 26, 2014

What a warm welcome at the home of Niue's high commissioner. We had drinks and snacks on the veranda, a welcoming talk, and insight into life on the island world.

Also, we went to a rally buffet dinner with dancing and singing with the locals and high school students. There was a great variety of food with local dishes in abundance. It was a festive night ashore for all!

(To read the complete blogs, go to worldsailing.guru/blogs.)

(May 20, 2014–May 24, 2014)   *Photo by Msdstefan at de.wikipedia (License CC BY-SA 2.0).*

- ## Alofi Moorage (Alofi Village, Cook Islands)

(Reference Only—Not for Navigation)

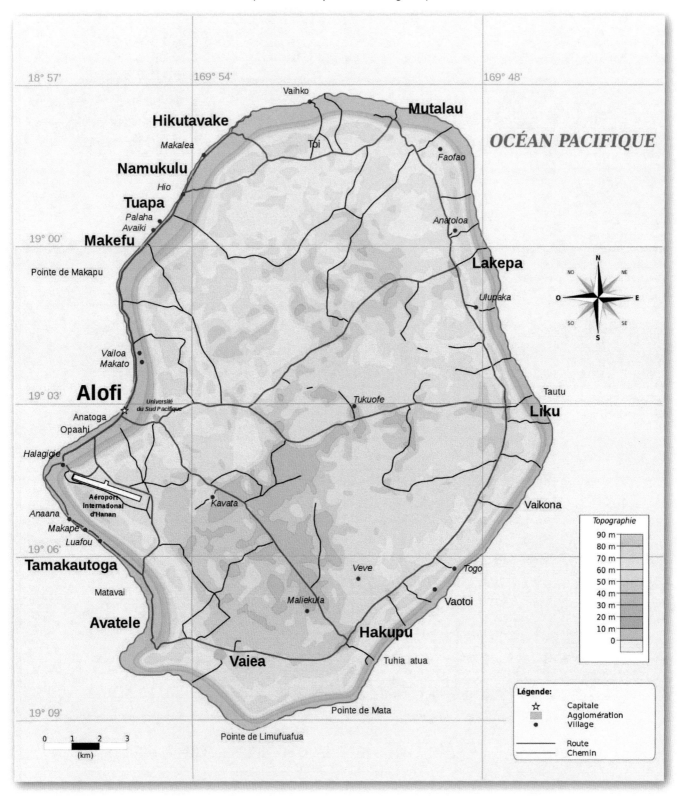

NIUE

Coordinates: 19°03' S, 169°55' W

Charts: BA 4630

Guides: *Ocean Passages & Landfalls* (Heikell and O'Grady)

South Pacific Anchorages (Clay)

Pacific Crossing Guide (RCC)

Landfalls of Paradise (Hinz)

Charlie's Charts of Polynesia (Wood)

In Brief

Pronounced "New Ay," Niue is a tiny, independent island country that is one of the Cook Islands in the South Pacific Ocean. However, it does maintain a close association with New Zealand.

Websites

http://www.niueisland.com

Customs and Immigration

All of the entry services are convenient at the port.

■ QuickFacts

— Time: UTC-11

— Language: English, Polynesian

— Currency: New Zealand dollars

— Weather/Climate: Tropical

— Tides/Currents: Two feet

Visas

There is no visa requirement for visits of fewer than 30 days, but you must show proof of funds and your transportation out.

Sea snakes are common around Niue, and we saw them on dinghy rides to the quay. Yes, they are highly venomous. Photo by FearlessRich (License CC BY 2.0).

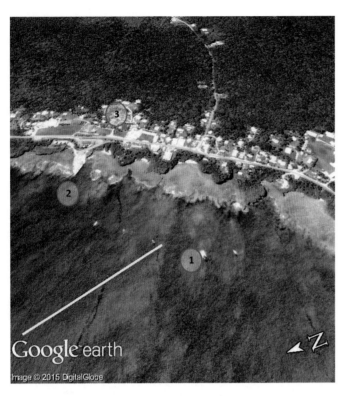

1. Mooring area
2. Dinghy landing/ship quay
3. Visitor center

Alofi Moorage

(Port of Entry)
Alofi Village, Cook Islands

Coordinates: 19°03' S, 169°55' W

Charts: BA 4630

Guides: *Ocean Passages & Landfalls* (Heikell
and O'Grady)
South Pacific Anchorages (Clay)
Pacific Crossing Guide (RCC)
Landfalls of Paradise (Hinz)
Charlie's Charts of Polynesia (Wood)

▪ QuickFacts

— Fuel: Jerry cans from the gas station
— Power: None
— Water: Jerry cans from shore, but water in the anchorage is clean enough for watermaker use

In Brief

Whatever your South Pacific dream, Niue seems to have it, from flocks of butterflies to underwater caverns. Alofi is the capital and very conveniently located.

Websites

www.niueisland.com

Approach

A daylight approach is recommended because boats are close together in the mooring field. Otherwise, navigation in is straightforward. Call Niue Radio on VHF channel 16.

At the Moorage

You can pick up any buoy for a mooring. These are provided by the Niue Yacht Club.

Take your dinghy to the concrete wharf, where you can unload passengers at the stairs and then use the crane to lift your dinghy out and place it on the dock. This is a bit of an adventure and can be quite exciting if there is a swell running.

Shoreside Services

The Niue Yacht Club has very helpful people with lots of information and advice.

Markets

There are two markets in the village within easy walking distance, but they are small, and the hours are limited.

Restaurants

There are a few cafés and bars.

Shopping

There are a few tourist items available, but almost anything you need will come via air from New Zealand.

Telephones

There is no cell service, but Niue prides itself in having free Wi-Fi throughout the island country.

Taxis

There is one taxi company. (See the tourist office below for rental cars.)

Airport and Airlines

The small airport is a short taxi ride from the moorage. Air New Zealand flies to Niue, but there is only one flight a week.

Accommodations

There are a few resorts available.

Things to Do and See

Niue Yacht Club

You can join the club. The cost is minimal for a lifetime membership, and you can get hats, T-shirts, and a burgee.

On Your Own

The tourist office near the dock has bicycles for rent and can arrange for rental cars. Then, you can visit all the island's sights.

The unusual dinghly landing arrangement at Niue. The mooring field is in the background, and dinghies are hoisted onto the quay by the crane. Photo by Ken Machtley and Cathy Siegismund, S/V Felicity, 2001.

Google earth

Data SIO, NOAA, U.S. Navy, NGA, GEBCO
Image Landsat
Image IBCAO

N

Passage Notes
(Niue to Fiji)

Expected Conditions

We had several days of spectacular downwind sailing to the Fiji Islands from Niue. We used a pretty wing-on-wing sail set with the whisker pole out. South Pacific Ocean sailing is great!

Places We Visited along the Way

None, we had commitments in Fiji.

Other Possible Stops

Tonga. This is a popular stop for many yachts crossing the South Pacific.

■ QuickFacts

— Mileage: 814 nm
— Duration: Six days
— Dates: May 24, 2014–May 30, 2014

Arrival

You cross the International Date Line on the way to Oneata Passage, where you enter the Fiji Islands. Be careful to adjust the date on any blog entries! After that, you cross the 180° meridian, where you stop going farther west and begin going less east!

We had to slow to arrive at Port Denarau in the daylight hours on May 30, 2014.

Caution: Fijian charts have variable accuracy, but the charts and lights through the break in the reef are good for main shipping routes, including to your port of entry.

S/V *Celebrate* Blog: The Edge of the Hemisphere in Fiji!

May 28, 2014

Kipling wrote that "East is East and West is West and never the twain shall meet." But we are not sure it's true.

Having sailed west for four months, we've just crossed the 180° meridian and entered the Eastern Hemisphere. It turns out we have gone east by going west!

Also, we have crossed the International Date Line and lost a day. Yesterday was Tuesday and we will arrive tomorrow, Friday, in Port Denarau. So that makes today what day? These are new confusions we haven't thought about before.

(To read the complete blogs online, go to worldsailing.guru/blogs.)

(May 30, 2014–July 4, 2014)   Celebrate *"dressed overall" at anchor in Fiji.*

- Port Denarau Marina (Denarau Island, Viti Levu Island)
- Musket Cove Marina/Moorage/Anchorage (Malolo Island)

(Reference Only—Not for Navigation)

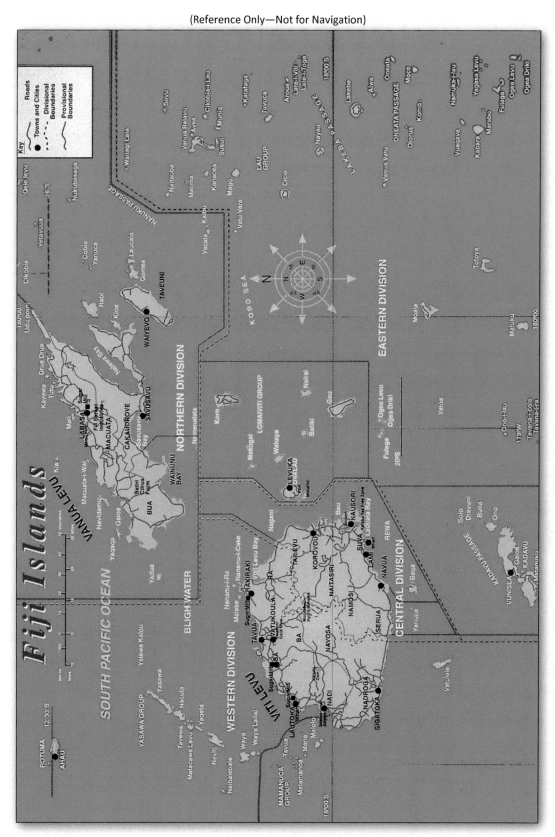

QuickStart Circumnavigation Guide

FIJI

Coordinates: 18°30′ S, 178°29′ W
(At Oneata Passage, for arrival in Fiji Island Group)
Charts: BA 2691, BA 441, BA 1670
Guides: *Ocean Passages & Landfalls* (Heikell and O'Grady)
South Pacific Anchorages (Clay)
Pacific Crossing Guide (RCC)
Landfalls of Paradise (Hinz)

In Brief

Fiji is a beautiful country of islands located between Vanuatu and New Caledonia in the South Pacific Ocean.

Fiji's rainforests are unique in having no harmful animals or insects. Fiji is also blessed with mountains, waterfalls, and beautiful vistas.

The major island is Viti Levu. Fiji is our favorite cruising stop and is favored by many cruisers because of its more than 300 islands, volcanic peaks, crystal clear lagoons, and outstanding wildlife.

Website

www.fijime.com

Customs and Immigration

You should visit the immigrations and customs website (www.frca.org.fj) and submit a form with all of your particulars to notify them of your arrival at least 48 hours in advance. Most common ports of entry are Savusavu, Suva, Levuka, and Lautoka.

Caution: Be sure to have your outbound clearance from your previous port! Fijian fines and inconveniences can be substantial.

Before we left Bora Bora, we had contacted an agent (Eli of the YachtHelp agency) to arrange for check-in for us and sent all the arrival documentation to her. Even though Port Denarau is *not* officially a port of entry, the agent can make the appropriate arrangements. We called YachtHelp on our sat phone an hour prior to arrival, and all the appropriate government representatives were at the boat within a few minutes of our arrival, and we were fully checked in within half an hour.

QuickFacts

— Time: UTC+12
— Language: English, Fijian
— Currency: Fiji dollars
— Weather/Climate: Tropical
— Tides/Currents: Five feet

Crews on other boats at the dock asked what sort of VIPs we were to have checked in so quickly.

Cruising Permit

A cruising permit is issued as part of the check-in process. Be sure to list all the places you might possibly like to visit, as amending the permit is more difficult than bypassing a destination.

Fiji is another tropical island paradise along the South Pacific "Coconut Milk Run." Photo by Jon-Eric Melsaeter (License CC BY 2.0).

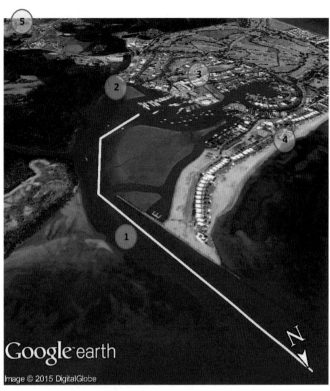

Image © 2015 DigitalGlobe

1. Well-marked entrance channel
2. Port Denarau Marina
3. Dockside shopping and restaurants
4. Hilton and other resorts down the beach
5. Town of Nadi

Port Denarau Marina

Denarau Island, Viti Levu

Coordinates: 17°46' S, 177°22' E

Charts: BA 1670

Guides: *Ocean Passages & Landfalls* (Heikell and O'Grady)

South Pacific Anchorages (Clay)

Pacific Crossing Guide (RCC)

Landfalls of Paradise (Hinz)

■ **QuickFacts**
— Fuel: Fuel dock. Small and may be draft-limited
— Power: 250V 50Hz
— Water: Potable water on the dock

In Brief

This luxury resort island is bridged to the main island of Fiji, Viti Levu, from which it is separated by a small, nonnavigable waterway. An ideal location for seeing Fiji and other areas by fast ferry.

Website

www.denaraumarina.com

Approach

We came through the break in the outer reef (about 10 nm south of the marina) just before daylight. The range marks and reef marks were in perfect agreement with the chart, as were the markers for the channel into the marina. We had no problems on entry.

Caution: Don't stray out of the marked marina channel, as areas of the lagoon dry at low tide.

Caution: This and other areas of Fijian waters used by commercial shipping have reasonably accurate charts. *In outlying areas of Fiji, charts are much less reliable.*

At the Marina

There is a very helpful staff and full-service superyacht capability.

At the head of the marina dock is a shopping complex with a small supermarket, many restaurants, and tour companies.

There is a Travelift and boatyard next to the marina, and boat parts can be flown in overnight from New Zealand.

Also, boats from New Zealand's premiere ocean race, Auckland to Fiji (ANZ Fiji), arrived at the marina while we were there. As one crew left their "gold-plated" ocean-racing boat, it seemed like there were 30 beefy guys to do the sailing. "How nice!" Cathy said.

Shoreside Services

Supermarkets

There is a small supermarket in the shopping complex at the head of the marina.

You can also take a city bus or taxi for a short ride into the town of Nadi for the marketplace.

Restaurants

There are many restaurants at the head of the marina with outdoor and inside tables. Here are a few:

Hard Rock Café—Great steaks and burgers.

Nadina—Wonderful Fijian food, lovely outdoor bayside seating, and live music. You can sample kava too.

Bone Fish—Nice seafood.

Telephones

You can get a local SIM card at the store at the marina.

Shopping

There is a shopping complex adjacent to the marina.

Taxis

Taxis are always available in the traffic circle near the ferry terminal at the head of the dock.

Airport and Airlines

Nearby Nadi Airport has numerous flights, primarily to Australia and New Zealand.

Accommodations

Many first-class resorts are available nearby, such as the Westin and Sofitel hotels.

Things to Do and See

On Your Own

Inside the ferry terminal and around the shopping complex, you can rent a car, arrange a tour of the island, plan rafting and dive trips, and find other entertainment.

You can take the Bula Bus ("bula" is Fijian for "hello") to any of a dozen resorts for additional dining and entertainment.

The Yasawa Islands form a chain to the northwest that includes the site where the *Blue Lagoon* movie was filmed.

After doing some preliminary navigation to the outer islands and figuring out how long it would take to sail there, we took the Yasawa Flyer (the fast catamaran passenger ferry) rather than take our own boat.

S/V *Celebrate* Blog: Idyllic Yasawa Islands All-Day Explorer Fast Catamaran Ferry Tour Starting in the Mamanuca Islands

June 16, 2014

We saw stunning scenery starting with some of the Mamanuca Islands, from South Sea Island to Volmo, showing steep volcanic cliffs. Then we cruised by the remote Yasawa Islands with beautiful white sand beaches and crystal-clear lagoons, including the famous *Blue Lagoon* movie site. There were a few cruising sailboats anchored in some of the bays, and it was a great opportunity to see where the really good spots to anchor were. It was a long day, with check-in at 7:45 a.m. at the Port Denarau Marina and the return at 6:30 p.m., but well worth it for sightseeing!

Passage Notes
(Port Denarau to Musket Cove)

Expected Conditions

It was an easy, two-hour sailing trip over to Musket Cove on Malolo Island with sunny weather.

Caution: for advice on reef positions, be sure to read the section on "Navigation by Google Maps" on page 151.

Places We Visited along the Way

None—it's too short a trip.

Other Possible Stops

Many islands with anchorages are available, including the extensive Yasawa Islands.

- **QuickFacts**
  — Mileage: 16 nm
  — Duration: Two hours
  — Date: June 17, 2014

Some cruisers enjoy Fiji so much they have spent a few years visiting many of the less-developed islands.

Arrival

We anchored at 17°46.211' S, 177°11.297' E, at the attractive Musket Cove on June 17, 2014. This is a swim-off-the-back-of-your-boat snorkeling place. One of our favorites!

1. *Entrance around the point. Note the center-channel rock!*
2. *Caution: these reefs vary from their charted positions!*
3. *Anchorage*
4. *Mooring balls*
5. *Marina and resort area*

In Brief

This is a wonderful island resort that welcomes cruising yachts. There is stern-tie dock space for a dozen yachts and a large mooring field plus anchorage area.

Website

www.musketcovefiji.com

Approach

Caution: Approach in the daytime with good light. Fiji's charts are poor at specific locations of coral reefs. See the chapter "Navigation by Google Maps" on page 151 for a comparison of the actual reef positions versus their charted locations. Reefs are marked with stakes, but without local knowledge, it is sometimes difficult to identify the safe side of the stake.

If you are going into the marina (which we did for fuel before heading for Vanuatu), be aware that we found a sandbar with its shallowest point (about 6 feet MLW) right at the marina entrance. Inside the marina, it was somewhat deeper.

Musket Cove Marina/Moorage/ Anchorage
Malolo Island

Coordinates: 17°46.211' S, 177°11.297' E

Charts: BA 1670

Guides: *Ocean Passages & Landfalls* (Heikell and O'Grady)
South Pacific Anchorages (Clay)
Pacific Crossing Guide (RCC)
Landfalls of Paradise (Hinz)

- ■ QuickFacts
  - — Fuel: Fuel dock. May be draft limited
  - — Power: 250V 50Hz
  - — Water: Potable water on the dock

We used the following waypoints:

17°47.108' S 177° 10.835' E
17°46.522' S 177° 10.717' E
17°46.295' S 177° 11.178' E (near our anchor spot)
17°46.270' S 177° 11.450' E (the marina entrance)

At the Marina/Moorings/Anchorage

As the marina is draft limited and the mooring balls are size limited, we anchored out and had a thoroughly enjoyable time at the resort. We are now members of the Musket Cove Yacht Club and have the interesting burgee to prove it.

Dockage at the marina is generally med-moor with your anchor going most of the way across the marina channel.

Shoreside Services

In the resort, there are several dining choices, pools, bars, a small supermarket, dive shops, and many activity choices.

Supermarket

There is a small supermarket at the resort.

Restaurant

There are several dining choices at the resort. Dick's was our favorite.

Telephones

Our Fiji SIM cards from Port Denerau continued to work.

Shopping

A nice boutique is at the resort.

Taxis

None that we were aware of.

Airport and Airlines

There is a grass strip, and you can charter a flight to Nadi, but the ferry is probably easier.

Accommodations

Stay at the resort or one of several others around the beach and across the island.

Things to Do and See

At the head of the dock (where you can land your dinghy) the "yacht club" is found inside at the dock office. There is also a dive shop and a complete resort activity center with bicycles, sailing dinghies, and beach activities.

Dive Trips with Subsurface Fiji

Also at the resort, Charlie took several dives with Subsurface Fiji. They picked him up from the boat at anchor and took him to spectacular reef dive sites.

Spectacular coral and fish are common in Fiji scuba dives. Photo by Tony Shih (License CC BY-ND 2.0).

S/V *Celebrate* Blog: Two Super Scuba Dives near Musket Cove, Fiji!

June 20, 2014

Subsurface Fiji conveniently picked me up at *Celebrate* for the two morning dives. Subsurface Fiji is located at Musket Cove Marina and did a great job of making the dive trip enjoyable. Out by Mana Island, we did a drift dive along a reef wall at the "Marketplace" dive site, where we saw black-tipped sharks and eagle rays. For our second dive at the "Barrel Head" site, there were spectacular colors of coral and many interesting reef fish I hadn't seen before. Also, the weather really cooperated with calm seas and super visibility for both dives. Another great adventure!

Charlie's Reef Diving at Musket Cove, Fiji!

June 28, 2014

We had more excellent diving with Subsurface Fiji. This trip showcased the "Charlie's Reef" dive site (my favorite!) and the Gotham City site.

Passage Notes
(Musket Cove, Fiji, to Tanna, Vanu-atu)

- **QuickFacts**
  - Mileage: 488 nm
  - Duration: Three days
  - Dates: July 4, 2014–July 7, 2014

Expected Conditions

After spectacular broad-reach winds the first night, winds dropped and backed.

We had departed Fiji early and hurried to Tanna as conditions were predicted to deteriorate, and winds reached 30–40 knots with rain the day after our arrival. The sailboats that arrived the day after us reported a "spirited" (rough) ride.

Places We Visited along the Way

None.

Other Possible Stops

- Mamma Nuka Islands (Fiji)
- Yasawa Islands (Fiji)
- Many other island anchorages available

Arrival

We anchored at 19°31.543′ S, 169°29.752′ E. We arrived at Tanna to a lovely welcome from the villagers of coconut milk served in coconuts.

S/V *Celebrate* Blog: Active Volcano Tour at Sunset and Village Welcome in Tanna, Vanuatu!

July 11, 2014

Wow! Standing at the rim of an active volcano is something not to be missed! Adrenaline rushes in you as the Mount Yasur cauldron spews up glowing lumps of lava at sunset from two places. A stunningly beautiful sight!

A lovely, lovely welcome from the villagers, complete with coconut milk served in coconuts, gifts for us made out of intricately woven leaves and grasses for hats, handbags, and satchels holding fruits and flowers. Also, there was singing and dancing and a tasty buffet dinner. We felt so warmly welcomed!

(To read the complete blogs, go to worldsailing.guru/blogs.)

VANUATU

(July 7, 2014–July 17, 2014)

Standing on the rim of Mount Yasur.

- Port Resolution Anchorage (Tanna Island)
- Yacht World Marina/Moorings (Port Vila, Efate Island)

(Reference Only—Not for Navigation)

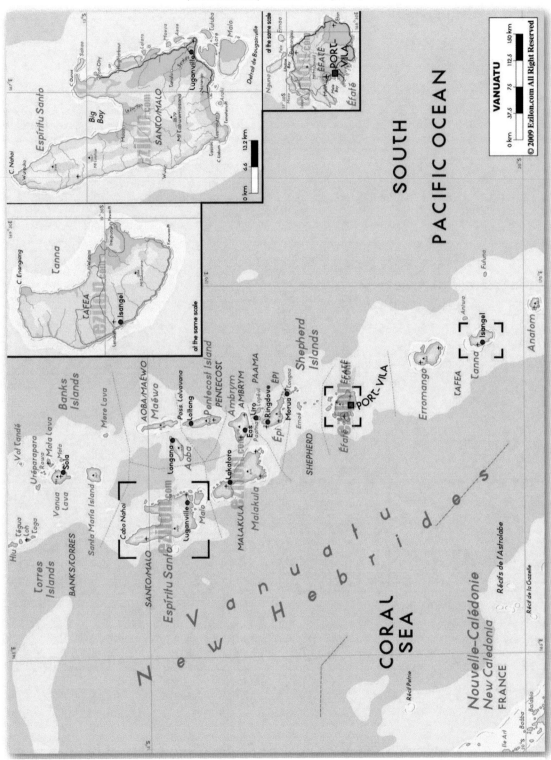

VANUATU

Coordinates: 19°31.543' S, 169°29.752' E
(Port Resolution Anchorage, Tanna Island)
Charts: BA 1494
Guides: *Ocean Passages & Landfalls* (Heikell and O'Grady)
South Pacific Anchorages (Clay)
Pacific Crossing Guide (RCC)
Landfalls of Paradise (Hinz)

In Brief

Considered a crossroads in the South Pacific Ocean, Vanuatu is a nation of volcanic islands located between New Caledonia and Fiji. A lovely people, mostly Melanesian, inhabit the islands.

Since we visited, a major cyclone (Pam) swept through Vanuatu, and there has been widespread devastation. We applaud the efforts of the many cruisers who helped rebuild.

Website

www.vanuatutourism.com

QuickFacts

— Time: UTC+11
— Language: English, French, Bislama
— Currency: Vatu
— Weather/Climate: Tropical
— Tides/Currents: Currents can be strong around the islands

Customs and Immigration

There are ports of entry at Lenakel on Tanna Island and in Port Vila on Efate Island. Quarantine officials must also clear yachts in.

In addition to the wonders on land, Vanuatu is another spectacular diving spot. Photo by Roderick Elme (License CC BY 2.0).

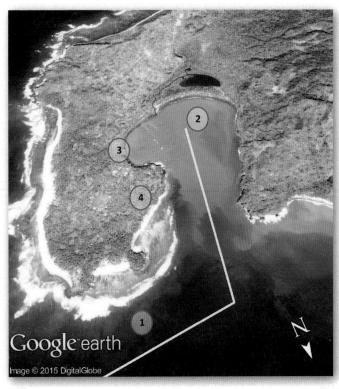

1. Leave plenty of clearance for off-lying rocks.
2. Anchorage
3. Dinghy landing on the beach. Watch out for the coral heads when entering the little bay (visible in this view).
4. Yacht club

Port Resolution Anchorage
(Port of Entry at Lenakal)
Tanna Island

Coordinates: 19°31.543' S, 169°29.752' W

Charts: BA 1494

Guides: *Ocean Passages & Landfalls*
 (Heikell and O'Grady)
 South Pacific Anchorages (Clay)
 Pacific Crossing Guide (RCC)
 Landfalls of Paradise (Hinz)

- ## QuickFacts
— Fuel: None
— Power: None
— Water: You can use your watermaker in the bay

In Brief

Tanna is a somewhat primitive island where the native population is very hospitable and is making great progress in balancing their nature-oriented way of life with outside forces and tourism.

Website

www.vanuatutourism.com

Approach

The approach into the bay is straightforward, but the chart is not high resolution enough to be very useful.

There is good holding in this spacious bay, but you need to keep a lookout with an eye on your depth sounder to show you the shallows and obstacles around the edges.

Caution: If approaching from the east, give the point a good half-mile clearance offshore to avoid off-lying rocks.

TIP: The chart is very low resolution, but augmenting your navigation with waypoints from Google Earth is practical. The bay is large, and holding is good.

At the Anchorage

There is a small tropical-style yacht club onshore with a rustic island bar. They'll help with tours and other island information.

The dinghy landing on the beach is down the hill from the yacht club, and it is easy and convenient.

Caution: Beware of near-surface coral on the way in.

Shoreside Services

Market
You can do some trading with locals for fresh fruit.

Supermarkets
None close by.

Restaurant
There are a bakery and dinner by reservation in a nearby family home.

Telephone
None.

Shopping

None nearby.

Taxis

Rides can sometimes be arranged with locals (ask at the yacht club).

Airport

The airport is across the island about an hour away by four-wheel drive.

Accommodations

None nearby.

Things to Do and See

Yacht Club

The club is happy to help you with tours and activities. Islanders with pickup trucks may be interested in giving you a tour.

Mount Yasur

A spectacular evening trip to Mount Yasur, the island's active volcano, was a high point of the entire cruise. This is a volcano where you can get as close as you like. You really get a feeling for the power of the earth's geological forces.

Tribal Dancers

You can watch the ancient tribal dances by arrangement.

Tanna tribal dancers. Photo by Carawa (License CC BY-ND 2.0).

The anchorage at Port Resolution is beautiful and well protected, and there was plenty of room for the entire World ARC fleet. Photo by World ARC.

My wife, Cathy, thought we were much too close to the volcano when she took this picture!

These custom-made palm-frond baskets are woven to hold almost anything. Photo by Bruce Tuten (License CC BY 2.0).

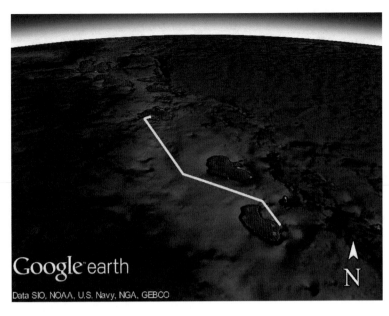

Passage Notes

(Port Resolution, Tanna Island, Vanuatu, to Port Vila, Efate Island, Vanuatu)

- ## QuickFacts
  - Mileage: 142 nm
  - Duration: One overnight
  - Dates: July 10, 2014–July 11, 2014

Expected Conditions

A wonderful motor-sail overnight to Port Vila.

We had a beautiful, moonlit night but had little wind and a 2-knot current against us. As we departed from Tanna, we could see the eruption of Mount Yasur glowing against the night sky.

Places We Visited along the Way

None.

Other Possible Stops

There is a possible anchorage on the west side of the island of Tafea.

Arrival

It was a quick overnight sail to the port city of Port Vila, arriving on July 11, 2014. You can contact Yachting World Marina for entry instructions on VHF channel 16.

Another farewell look at spectacular Mount Yasur, which is visible as a glow in the sky as you sail away from Tanna. Photo by Jon Andrew J Swann (License CC BY-SA 3.0).

1. *Cloud (not a reef) on the aerial photo*
2. *Shallows in this area with narrow channels suggest following the marina launch carefully.*
3. *Mooring field*
4. *Yachting World Marina*

In Brief

Port Vila is a busy capital port city on Efate Island with a vibrant economy.

Website

www.yachtingworld-vanuatu.com

Approach

The chart into Port Vila is reasonably detailed.

Caution: Pay attention to the low water level at the entry and the overhead cable. Call Yachting World Marina on VHF channel 16, and they will send a launch to lead you in, as the deep part of the marina entrance is quite narrow.

At the Marina

There is a seawall tie-up, and mooring balls are available. Also, the staff is very helpful.

Yachting World Marina/Moorings

(Port of Entry)
Port Vila, Efate Island

Coordinates: 17°44' S, 168°18' W

Charts: BA 1494

Guides: *Ocean Passages & Landfalls*
(Heikell and O'Grady)
South Pacific Anchorages (Clay)
Pacific Crossing Guide (RCC)
Landfalls of Paradise (Hinz)

■ **QuickFacts**
— Fuel: Fuel dock next to the marina
— Power: 250V 50Hz
— Water: Potable water on the dock

Shoreside Services

Market

Excellent fresh produce is available at the large market in town. It is about a 10-minute walk.

Supermarket

A few smaller markets are on the main street, and there is the Au Bon Marché with a good selection. Take a taxi for a quick five-minute ride.

Restaurant

A wide variety of restaurants is close to the marina on Main Street.

Telephones

We did not arrange SIM cards, but cell phone service is available.

Shopping

There was wonderful shopping all around town. There are interesting local curios as well as the usual T-shirts.

Taxis

Taxis are always available in front of the hotel next to the marina, but you should agree on a price before starting off.

Airport and Airlines

Bauerfield is Vanuatu's international airport with flights to New Zealand, Australia, and locally to other islands.

Accommodations

There is a nice hotel with a nice restaurant and casino next to the marina. It's great for lunch on the deck on a sunny day.

Things to Do and See

Tourist Office

The tourist office on the main street can arrange excellent day tours of the island. These tours can include visits to demonstrations of native villages and customs.

We saw fire walking on our tour.

Diving

There is a dive shop next the marina with amazing dives available.

Here is the mooring field of the Yachting World Marina in the foreground with the dock at the right-hand side. Photo by Phillip Capper (License CC BY 2.0).

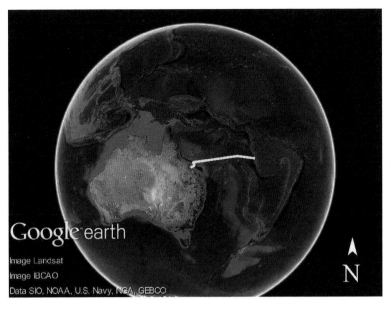

Passage Notes

(Port Vila, Vanuatu, to Mackay, Australia)

- **QuickFacts**
  — Mileage: 1,202 nm
  — Duration: Six days
  — Dates: July 17, 2014–July 23, 2014

Expected Conditions

There was plenty of wind. We sailed with the full mainsail and unrolled the full genoa on the whisker pole. We saw a few whales and had pretty nights with full, bright moons and sunny days. It was stunning sailing!

Places We Visited along the Way

None.

Other Possible Stops

New Caledonia—A French island with excellent tourism.

New Zealand—If you are choosing to extend your trip for an entire season, you can take the Southern Hemisphere summer in New Zealand. It lies south of the usual hurricane tracks.

Arrival

We went through the Great Barrier Reef at Hydrographers Passage at daybreak to make our Australian landfall. We arrived at the marina well after dark that evening (July 23, 2014).

Australian charts have excellent accuracy, but be sure to use larger-scale charts. The chart that shows this entire route makes no indication of the intervening ocean reefs, including the Great Barrier Reef.

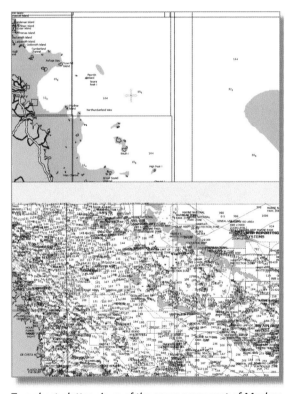

Two chart plotter views of the same area west of Mackay. Although the zoom level is only slightly different, the Great Barrier Reef (green in the lower image) doesn't show at all in the upper chart. This illustrates the importance of zooming in to check all routes carefully.

S/V *Celebrate* Blog: Helicopter AIS, Glacier Bay-like Humpbacks, and *Sophie*'s Storybook!

August 17, 2014

We are just passing Cairns on our passage up to Darwin, Australia, from Mackay. The Mackay Marina people were so good to us that we gave them three large gift bags of cookies and other treats. They gave us the *Sophie* book about a famous dog owned by Bridget at the marina. They were such great people!

Also, we saw a helicopter AIS icon flying around for the first time on our electronic chart. It looks like a helicopter shadow moving around. There is much more detail than the boat icons.

We have had two more humpback whale sightings. It reminds us of our sailing trip into Glacier Bay, Alaska, with many humpback whales around. They are *big*!

(To read the complete blogs, go to worldsailing.guru/blogs.)

(July 23, 2014–September 2, 2014)

Kangaroos. Photo by Pan BK (License CC BY-SA 3.0).

- Mackay Marina and Shipyard (Mackay, Queensland)
- Tipperary Waters Marina (Darwin, Northern Territory)

(Reference Only—Not for Navigation)

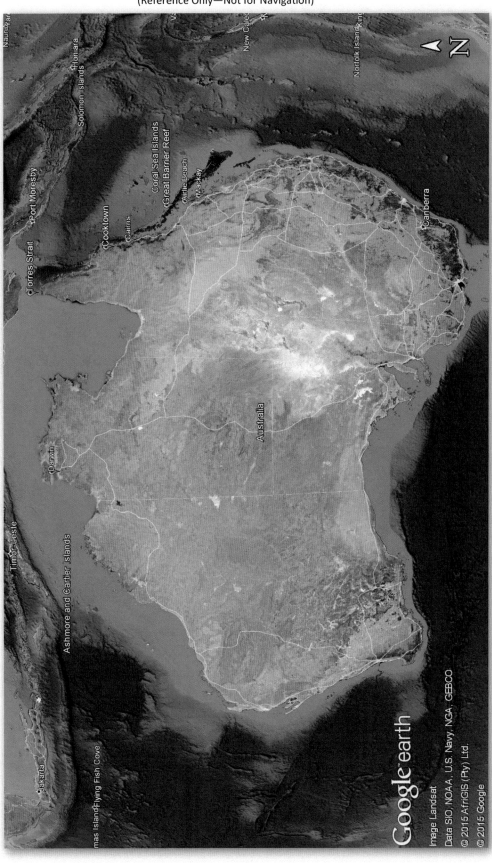

AUSTRALIA

Coordinates: 21°06′ S, 149°15′ E (Entering Mackay)

Charts: AUS 251, AUS 252, AUS26

Guides: *Ocean Passages & Landfalls* (Heikell and O'Grady)

Pacific Crossing Guide (RCC)

100 Magic Miles (Colfelt)

Cruising the Coral Coast (Lucas)

Torres Strait Passage Guide (Hellewell)

In Brief

Australia is a *vast* country. It is about the size of the continental United States but with about one-tenth of the population. There is plenty of room and lots to see and do. The eastern coast is populated and developed, but the northern coast you'll sail past is almost empty.

Caution: Again, Australian charts have excellent accuracy, but be sure to use the larger-scale charts. The chart-plotter view (page 69) showing longer routes *makes no indication of the intervening ocean reefs including the Great Barrier Reef.*

After your trip through the Pacific and many island nations with varying degrees of development, Mackay and Darwin will be opportunities for US-style shopping for clothes, provisions, and boat parts.

Caution: Beware of the risk of saltwater crocodiles ("salties"), which frequently attack and kill people swimming within their territory. Heed the warnings, and don't swim in near-shore waters.

Websites

www.Australia.com
www.immi.gov.au

Customs and Immigration

Australian entrance requirements can be daunting, and some preplanning is necessary to smooth the way.

Read this information and take it seriously. The Australian authorities take their rules seriously as well:

https://www.border.gov.au/Trav/Ente/Avia/Maritime/Requirements-for-yachts-and-pleasure-craft

Each visitor must have a valid passport *and* a visa or Electronic Travel Authority, which you must obtain online here:

▪ QuickFacts

— Time: UTC+10 to UTC+8
— Language: English
— Currency: Australian dollar
— Weather/Climate: Varies
— Tides/Currents: Vary and can be quite large

https://www.eta.immi.gov.au/ETAS3/etas

You must provide 48 hours' advance notice of arrival (usually via e-mail).

On arrival you must initially tie up at the customs dock and await inspection. In addition to the usual Customs and Immigration, your yacht will likely be inspected for drugs and weapons. Sometimes the inspectors will use dogs, but the dogs have booties to protect your boat.

The most problematic inspection will often be by the quarantine department, which, for all practical purposes, does not allow any fresh food to be brought in and will confiscate, for disposal, anything that violates their regulations. Furthermore, when you enter into Darwin, there will also be a decontamination process as protection against migration of certain sea creatures. Your boat will be inspected by divers, who will put biocides in your through hulls, and your boat cannot be moved for most of a day.

After the entry procedures are complete, you are free to explore the wonders of Australia.

Cruising Permits

Cruising permits are valid for 12 months and can be applied for on arrival.

1. Breakwater
2. Sugar terminal
3. Marina, hotel, and restaurants
4. Boatyard and boat services
5. Downtown Mackay

Mackay Marina and Shipyard

(Port of Entry)
Mackay, Queensland

Coordinates: 21°06′ S, 149°15′ E

Charts: AUS251, AUS252

Guides: *Ocean Passages & Landfalls* (Heikell and O'Grady)

Pacific Crossing Guide (RCC)

100 Magic Miles (Colfelt)

Cruising the Coral Coast (Lucas)

Torres Strait Passage Guide (Hellewell)

▪ QuickFacts

— Fuel: Fuel dock next to marina
— Power: 250V 50Hz
— Water: Potable water on the dock
— Tidal Range: Caution: tides up to 16 feet
— Time: UTC+10

In Brief

Just north of Brisbane, Australia, is Mackay (pronounced "McEye" by most inhabitants). Mackay has a wonderful, picturesque landscape with numerous acres of sugarcane and the occasional platypus.

Website

www.destinationqueensland.com

Approach

Mackay has a massive harbor, and the marina shares the breakwater with the sugar terminal, while the even larger coal terminal is to the south. The field of ships anchored out rivals the Panama Canal.

Accordingly, the entry is well marked and straightforward, except for possible ship traffic. After going through the breakwater to the sugar terminal, follow the breakwater south to enter the marina, and head for the customs docks to await clearance in and a slip assignment.

At the Marina

The marina has protected floating docks, all the usual services, and a small chandlery. The adjacent haul-out and yard facility can do all repairs and have parts imported in a reasonably reliable timeframe.

Shoreside Services

Supermarket

In town at the mall, there are two large supermarkets.

Restaurants

A variety of restaurants are located right on the marina, everything from fast food to gourmet.

Telephones

You can get a local SIM card at the mall or at the marina. Because of the tidal range, the cell coverage was marginal for us when our boat slip was at low tide.

Shopping

A great selection of almost everything is at the mall.

For the boat, there is a chandlery at the marina and another downtown. Also, many of the shipyard service shops can arrange to supply anything you need.

Taxis

The marina office can call you a taxi for the ride into town. They also have a few cars and motorbikes available for rental.

Airport and Airlines

The Mackay Airport is about a 20-minute taxi ride from the marina and offers domestic flights with connections to Brisbane or Sydney for international flights.

Accommodations

The Clarion Hotel overlooks the marina.

Things to Do and See

Tourist Office

The tourist office is in the Town Hall Visitor Center downtown.

On Your Own

There is so much to see on the east coast of Australia that you could spend years. The wildlife is unique, and the scenery is exquisite.

Great Barrier Reef and Diving

The Great Barrier Reef lies 50–75 miles offshore. You will have gone through it on your way to Mackay and may wish to return for the great diving and snorkeling. An organized dive tour from the mainland may be the fastest and safest way for you to scuba.

Eungella National Park

Eungella National Park is a rainforest about an hour's drive from Mackay. We spotted a platypus in the river there.

The platypus is one of many species uniqe to Australia. Photo by Peter Scheunis (License CC BY 1.0).

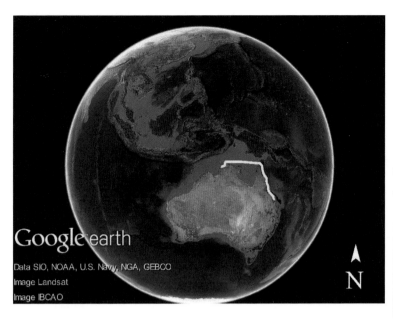

Passage Notes

(Mackay, Australia, to Darwin, Australia)

- **QuickFacts**
  — Mileage: 1,565 nm
  — Duration: Nine days
  — Dates: August 16, 2014–August 25, 2014

Expected Conditions

To start, we had smooth waters and not much wind. After passing Cairnes and fueling at Cooktown, we headed through Albany Passage, into Endeavor Strait and the Arafura Sea. Finally, we had perfect wind for a beam reach for two days. Then, on to Darwin via Howard Channel and Clarence Strait.

Because the first part of the passage is inside the Great Barrier Reef, you'll seldom find rough seas, but the shipping traffic is very heavy. Then, the long passage across the northern coast can be a wonderful sailing reach.

Places We Visited along the Way

Cooktown for Fuel

Cooktown is a convenient short stop with an anchorage and a few dock spaces. It is the last stop with any marine services before rounding the corner through to Torres Strait and the long westward leg to Darwin (nearly 1,000 miles).

Whitehaven Beach is a popular stop on Whitsunday Island. Photo by slug69 (License CC BY-SA 2.0).

Caution: The markers were moved about by a recent cyclone and were off station. The charted position of the channel was correct.

Other Possible Stops

Whitsunday Islands—With many wonderful places to anchor out and visit, you'll want to plan on a few stops here on your way north.

Airlie Beach—This is a great sailing capital that may be a valuable visit for sail, rigging, and sailing-specific repairs. It has several marinas and a huge anchorage area.

Cairnes—An excellent stop with major boat facilities and access to the Great Barrier Reef.

Thursday Island—Located in the Torres strait, this island is a popular stop with some cruisers but entails additional quarantine issues upon arrival at Darwin.

Papua New Guinea—This is a wonderful cruising destination in its own right.

Arrival

Our arrival was at dawn on August 25, 2014, at Darwin for immediate pest treatment at the quarantine/fuel dock at Cullen Bay. In the late afternoon, we proceeded to Tipperary Waters Marina through the locks that regulate its water level.

Tipperary Waters Marina

(Port of Entry)
Darwin, Northern Territory

Coordinates: 12°27′ S, 130°49′ E

Charts: AUS 26

Guides: *Ocean Passages & Landfalls* (Heikell and O'Grady)

Google earth

Image © 2015 TerraMetrics
Image © 2015 Sinclair Knight Merz & Fugro

1. *Decontamination and fuel dock outside the locks of Cullen Bay Marina.*
2. *Tipperary Waters Marina*
3. *Downtown Darwin*

In Brief

Darwin is the largest city on Australia's North Coast, and, with about 150,000 inhabitants, you get some idea of the vast emptiness of northern Australia.

Website

www.tipperarywatersmarina.com

Approach

Consult your tide and current tables. With proper timing, you can ride the current stream in through the Van Diemen Gulf and save hours of sailing time. The channels through Clarence Strait are well marked, but watch out for current set.

On entering the Darwin area, you'll first stop at the fuel dock outside the Cullen Bay Marina for the decontamination procedures, which will require most of a day. Then proceed around the peninsula and up the well-marked creek. Call the marina lockmaster to arrange to lock through into the marina. The lock is not accessible at low tide, so consult with the marina prior to approach.

QuickFacts

— Fuel: Fuel dock at Cullen Marina
— Power: 250V 50Hz
— Water: Potable water on the dock
— Tidal Range: Up to 25 feet. Caution: So large that marinas are protected by locks
— Time: UTC+9:30

At the Marina

The marina staff are quite happy to help with information on tours and activities.

Sailmaker

One block from the marina entrance is a sailmaker. We loaded our mainsail into a shopping cart and wheeled it over for minor repairs.

Shoreside Services

Supermarket

A few miles away at the city center, there is a nice supermarket, which is great for a major reprovisioning before heading into the Indian Ocean.

Restaurants

Several restaurants are available at the marina area, from a deli-style outside hamburger stand with bar to a nice Thai restaurant.

Telephone

Keep your local SIM card from Mackay; it may still work. Ours did.

Shopping

There is plenty of shopping available at the city center.

Taxis

The marina office will arrange a taxi for you.

Airport and Airlines

Darwin International Airport has international flights with Quantas and Virgin Blue airlines.

Accommodations

There is a wide range of hotels.

Things to Do and See

Tourist Office

Visit the Darwin Regional Tourist Information Center.

Street Goods Market

A visit to the Smith Street pedestrian mall can introduce you to aboriginal art as well as local pearls and gems.

National Parks

Darwin is practically surrounded by national parks. Litchfield National Park is noted for its waterfalls and abundant wildlife. The enormous Kakadu National Park is home to aboriginal rock-art paintings.

Ayers Rock/Uluru

We took a plane to Alice Springs and then took a bus tour of Uluru (previously called Ayers Rock). You can take the Ghan train along a similar route, and it's an excellent rail trip through the Australian outback.

Prehistoric aboriginal art work at Ayers Rock/Uluru. Photo by Richard Riley (License CC BY 2.0).

Amazing Ayers Rock/Uluru Side Tour from Alice Springs, Australia!

September 2, 2014

After welcoming Peter on board *Celebrate* in Darwin and meeting his lovely friends Paula and Diane for a great Greek dinner, we were ready to fly out to Alice Springs as a sightseeing base for an all-day bus tour to Ayers Rock (now called Uluru). At the amazing "rock," we were able to take several walks around the base with its ancient aboriginal paintings. Also, we were able to visit another huge rock formation nearby called Kata Tjuta. We finished the day with a sunset view of Ayers Rock with many changing colors and a festive BBQ with a glass of champagne. What magnificent sights!

Our visit to Ayers Rock/Uluru in the Australian Outback.

Passage Notes
(Darwin, Australia, to Bali)

Expected Conditions

From Darwin to Bali, the trip is often characterized by light winds and some motoring to start. After a few days, we had 20-knot trade winds and had to reduce sail in order to arrive in the daytime, as Bali International Marina at Benoa Harbor is closed overnight.

Places We Visited along the Way

None.

Other Possible Stops

Lombok, Indonesia.

- **QuickFacts**
  - Mileage: 925 nm
  - Duration: Six days
  - Dates: September 2, 2014–September 8, 2014

On Arrival

Before taking care of clearances around town on arrival (September 8, 2014), we were able to have an eggs Benedict breakfast at the Bali International Marina restaurant.

Mount Agung is one of the famous sights of Bali about 30 miles from the harbor. Photo by Jesse Wagstaff (License CC BY 2.0).

S/V *Celebrate* Blog: Bali Blessing

September 14, 2014

Before leaving the dock at Bali International Marina, *Celebrate* and her crew were blessed by local guide Aasa and his wife. The ceremony, which many boats participated in, involved a prayer, a floral offering, and a flower placed behind our ears. This, together with lots of smiles and farewells, made our departure very special. Once out at the start, we threw more offerings into the sea to help make it a safe and enjoyable passage. The blessings appear to be working, as we are enjoying a good breeze, more than the light winds the weather forecast had promised.

(To read the complete blogs, go to worldsailing.guru/blogs.)

BALI

(September 8, 2014–September 14, 2014)   Celebrate's *crew being blessed by a local guide.*

- Bali International Marina, Benoa Harbor

(Reference Only—Not for Navigation)

BALI (INDONESIA)

Coordinates: 8°44′ S, 115°12′ E

Charts: BA 946

Guides: *Ocean Passages & Landfalls* (Heikell and O'Grady)

In Brief

Bali is one of the numerous islands that make up Indonesia. Bali Island is 90 by 48 miles and borders the Bali Sea to the north and the Indian Ocean to the south.

Website

www.balitourismboard.org

Customs and Immigration

Checking into Bali can be an adventure with lots of paperwork and stamps. You'll need clearance from:

- Health
- Customs
- Immigration
- Indonesian Navy
- Benoa port captain

All of these organization have offices in different locations, and they must be visited in the appropriate order. Fortunately, the marina is a great help. With their help and map, you can be checked into Indonesia in a morning.

▪ QuickFacts

— Time: UTC+8
— Language: Bahasa and Balinese (some English in tourist areas)
— Currency: Indonesian rupiah (Rp)
— Weather/Climate: Tropical
— Tides/Currents: Currents can be strong around the islands

Visas

Citizens of most countries, including Americans, can secure a visa for 30 days upon arrival. Payment can be made in local currency or US dollars.

Cruising Permit

The Bali Marina will process the cruising permit, called a CAIT, for you.

Spectacular Bali sunset. Photo by Haley-H (License CC BY 2.0).

1. *Bali International Marina*
2. *Benoa Harbor (ships)*
3. *City of Denpasar*

Bali International Marina

(Port of Entry)
Benoa Harbor

Coordinates: 8°44' S, 115°12' E

Charts: BA946

Guides: *Ocean Passages & Landfalls*
 (Heikell and O'Grady)

- **QuickFacts**
— Fuel: Fuel dock next to marina
— Power: 250V 50Hz
— Water: Caution: water on the dock is not potable, and watermaker use is not advised
— Currents: Can be greater than 1 knot, as small tidal fluctuation is funneled through the breaks between islands

In Brief

Nearby highlights of Bali include rice paddies and Hindu temples. The city is a bustling metropolis with serious traffic.

Websites

www.balimarina.com

Approach

The channel into the harbor and the marina is well marked, but you'll begin to feel the tidal currents 30 miles from the island and they are swift enough through the channel to require vigilance. You should call the marina on VHF channel 77.

At the Marina

There is a very helpful staff, and it is a full-service marina. There is 24-hour security and video surveillance, but be mindful of your belongings and boat equipment.

Shoreside Services

Market

The marketplace has unique local fruits and vegetables.

Balinese dance is beautiful, unique, and worth a special tour. Photo by kayugee (License CC BY-ND 2.0).

Supermarkets

There are a few minimarts within walking distance, but a taxi ride will take you to a supermarket in Denpasar.

Restaurants

There is a restaurant at the head of the dock and several others within walking distance.

Shopping

In Denpasar, there is a wide variety.

Telephones

You can get a local SIM card in the store at the marina.

Taxis

Taxis can be arranged by the marina.

Airport and Airlines

Nearby Ngurah Ral International Airport has direct international flights.

Accommodations

Many hotels are available, including some world-class luxury resorts.

Things to Do and See

Tourist Office

The marina office can help to arrange excellent day tours of the island through a visiting travel agent. Tours can include rice paddies and visits to Hindu temples.

On Your Own

A taxi ride into the city of Denpasar to go shopping is an adventure in itself!

Resorts

Bali has a huge tourist industry offering accommodations and dining at all levels of luxury and pocketbook.

Diving

There are numerous small dive companies to take you to a variety of beautiful dive spots.

This wonderful Hindu temple, Puar Ulun Danu Bratan, is on the shore of Lake Bratan near the center of the island. Photo by Joan Campderrós-i-Canas (License CC BY-SA 2.0).

A fruit vendor at the market in Denpasar.

Bali rice paddies are terraced up the hillside. Photo by Jon-notic (License CC BY-ND 2.0).

Passage Notes
(Bali to Cocos (Keeling) Islands)

Expected Conditions

We flew through the Indian Ocean at up to 10 knots with all our sails up. Night watches were busy with a lookout for local fishing boats. With the addition of a favorable current, we had a very fast run.

Places We Visited along the Way

None.

Some Potential Stops

Christmas Island—An Australian island with excellent tourism about halfway between Bali and Cocos (Keeling).

Arrival

We dropped anchor at 12°05.575' S, 96°52.884' E at stunning Port Refuge anchorage on September 20, 2014—a perfect tropical island scene.

- **QuickFacts**
  - Mileage: 1,029 nm
  - Duration: Six days
  - Dates: September 14, 2014–September 20, 2014

Christmas Island is famous for its red crabs. Photo by John Tan (License CC BY 2.0).

S/V *Celebrate* Blog: Sharks!!!! Port Refuge on Direction Island at Cocos (Keeling)

September 20, 2014

At about 7:00 a.m. local time, we arrived safely in Cocos (Keeling). The wind died as we made our approach, and in clear daylight we could pick up the leading navigation marks. We followed the waypoints of a previous World ARC participant, which got us into the anchorage without a problem, although at one point there was no more than a foot under the keel!

There is beautiful turquoise water, palm trees, and a sandy beach to add to the scene! We have to wait onboard until this afternoon for Australian customs to clear us, so it is time for a welcoming beer, and then we are off to discover the sights above and below the water.

(To read the complete blogs, go to worldsailing.guru/blogs.)

INDIAN OCEAN

(September 20, 2014–October 31, 2014)   Celebrate *at anchor in Port Refuge at Cocos (Keeling). Photo by World ARC.*

- Port Refuge Anchorage (Direction Island, Cocos (Keeling) Islands)
- Le Caudan Waterfront Marina (Port Louis, Mauritius Island)
- Le Port Harbor (Réunion Island)

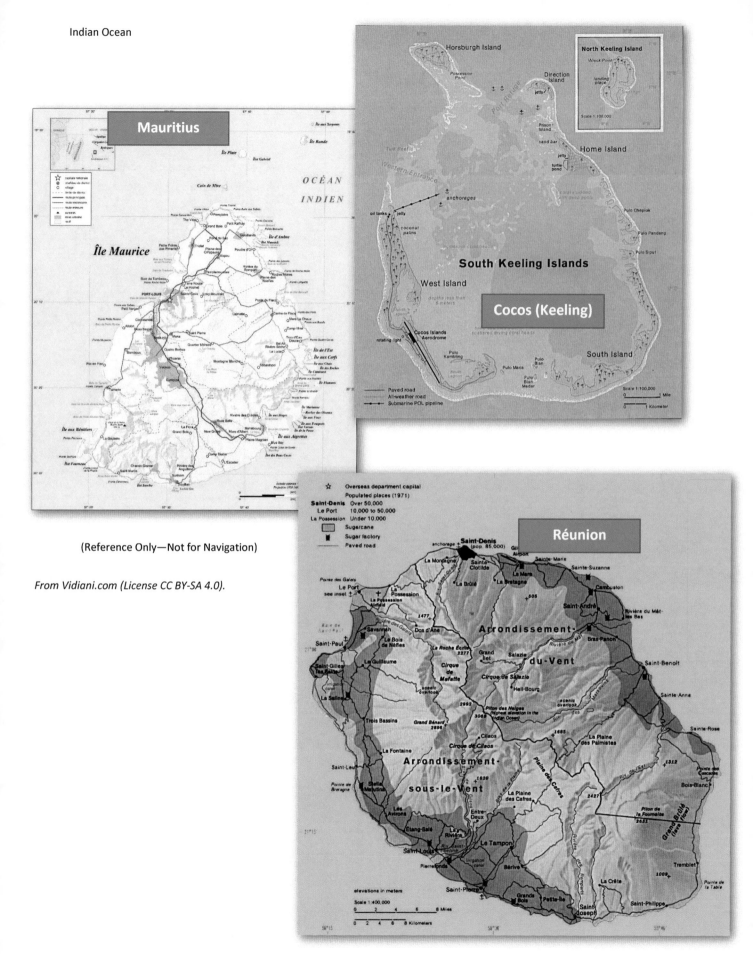

Mauritius

Cocos (Keeling)

Réunion

(Reference Only—Not for Navigation)

From Vidiani.com (License CC BY-SA 4.0).

Cocos (Keeling) Islands

(Port of Entry)
Port Refuge Anchorage, Direction Island

Coordinates: 12°05.575' S, 96°52.884' E

Charts: AUS 606, AUS 607

Guides: *Indian Ocean Cruising Guide* (Heikell)

Ocean Passages & Landfalls (Heikell and O'Grady)

1. *Usual entry route*
2. *Deeper route but somewhat harder to find*
3. *Direction Island*
4. *Home Island*
5. *West Island*

▪ QuickFacts

— Time: UTC + 6:30
— Language: English and Malay
— Currency: Australian dollar
— Weather/Climate: Tropical
— Tides/Current: Three feet
— Fuel: None (a long dinghy/ferry ride to fill jerry cans)
— Power: None
— Water: Clear for watermaker use

In Brief

This wonderful island group is an Australian territory, although only one flight per week connects them. It's named Cocos (Keeling) by act of law but is the only island we are aware of with parentheses.

Cocos (Keeling) consists of several islands (totaling less than 6 square miles of land area and a reported population of 659) surrounding a large lagoon, which is not generally navigable, and anchoring is allowed only at Port Refuge at the bay of Direction Island. From there it is a (usually) bumpy, several-mile dinghy ride to Home Island, which is generally populated by Malay immigrants, and a half-hour ferry ride from there to the more Australian West Island.

Website

cocoskeelingislands.com.au

Customs and Immigration

Although officially the entry rules and quarantine requirements are identical to Australia proper, in practice the process is much easier. With advance notification and recent entry into Australia, set your anchor and call the Cocos Police on VHF channel 16. They will arrange to send a launch to your boat with the appropriate officials to check you in. The process is not instant, as the launch has to come from West Island, 5 miles away.

Visas

All crew need to comply with Australian visa requirements, but your Electronic Travel Authority may not have expired yet.

Approach

You should plan on arriving at Cocos during daylight hours. The anchorage entrance is shown in the satellite photo.

Enter the lagoon from the north and the entry to the anchorage will be clear, but the most direct route carries only 6 feet of water at low tide. A somewhat more circuitous route through a break in the reef south of the anchorage (also shown on the map) is used by the ferry once a week and is marked by buoys that appear confusing as you approach from the west. There are a few buoys not related to the channel. and remember, red is to port.

At the Anchorage

The anchorage is idyllic but sometimes choppy. A short dinghy ride or swim gets you ashore to Direction Island on the beach or the back of the ferry dock.

Shoreside Services

Supermarkets

There is a nice smaller supermarket with an Asian character on Home Island, which you can dinghy to—about 2 nm of potentially choppy water. On West Island, which you reach by ferry (no dinghy landing), there is a larger market with a more Western flavor that will also take special orders airfreighted from Australia.

Restaurants

West Island has a few restaurants, cafes, and bars. Home Island has no alcohol, as it is largely Muslim, but there are a few cafes.

Shopping

There are various tourist shops on West Island.

Telephones

Your Australian SIM card should work in Cocos (Keeling).

Taxis

Taxis are available on West Island but are more or less ad hoc, as one would expect with the overall population being less than 1,000. Everything on Home Island is within walking distance of the dinghy dock.

Airport and Airlines

West Island Airport has flights from Perth, Australia, every few days.

Accommodations

There are a few small motels on West Island.

Things to Do and See

Tourist Office

There is a tourist office on West Island that can be accessed by phone from the anchorage. They can help arrange tours and dive trips.

On Your Own

The islands are gorgeous, and just snorkeling, swimming, or walking around exploring is inspirational. Also, take a walk on the beach.

Direction Island

Direction Island has a nice nature walk and signs detailing Cocos (Keeling)'s strategic position as a communications relay station during World War II.

West Island

- A community farm tour—Visit a group creating sea salt and palm oil to make beauty products and condiments.
- Clam farm tour—We particularly enjoyed seeing the tanks where clams are raised in various colors for the international aquarium trade.
- Art tour—The large beached boat, made into an art gallery and studio, specializes in artwork created from ocean debris, which largely floats in from Bali.

The main road on West Island isn't very big, but it doesn't have far to go. Photo by David Stanley (License CC BY 2.0).

Passage Notes
(Cocos (Keeling) to Mauritius)

- **QuickFacts**
  - Mileage: 2,377 nm
  - Duration: 13 days
  - Dates: September 29, 2014–October 12, 2014

Expected Conditions

At 2,377 miles, this is one of a circumnavigation's longer passages. On our way to Mauritius, we were going 10 knots+ with days of 30-knot winds and a series of squalls. It was a little bumpy at times, but fast!

Also, flying fish jumped aboard everywhere, and there were stars galore at night.

Places We Visited along the Way

None.

Other Possible Stops

Rodrigues Island can be a pleasant stop about 400 miles east of Mauritius. Although it's a part of Mauritius, you still have to clear in and out.

For those on a more leisurely trip, you can spend the Indian Ocean cyclone season north of the equator on the coast of India and the Maldives.

Arrival

We played our "Celebration" song at arrival on October 12, 2014. What a beautiful island we have come to.

Round the north side of Mauritius and enter the Port Louis harbor from the west.

We sailed toward some spectacular Indian Ocean sunsets. Photo by Miwok (Public Domain).

Mauritius Island

(Port of Entry)
Le Caudan Waterfront Marina, Port Louis

Coordinates: 20°09' S, 57°29' E

Charts: BA 712, BA 711

Guides: *Indian Ocean Cruising Guide*
(Heikell)
Ocean Passages & Landfalls
(Heikell and O'Grady)

- ## QuickFacts
  — Time: UTC + 4
  — Language: English and French
  — Currency: Mauritius rupee
  — Weather/Climate: Tropical
  — Tides/Current: Insignificant
  — Fuel: A tank trailer can be brought to your boat
  — Power: 220V 50Hz
  — Water: Potable water at the dock

1. Marina
2. Customs dock
3. Caudan waterfront development

In Brief

Mauritius is a mountainous volcanic island with a modern infrastructure and over one million in population.

Websites

www.tourism-mauritius.mu
www.caudan.com

Customs and Immigration

Yachts clearing in at Port Louis may be asked to clear with Customs and Immigration before berthing. The customshouse is in the northeast corner of the harbor, with a gray slate roof.

Visas

Visas are not required for US citizens, and you can check online at:

www.maurinet.com/tourist_information/visa_information.

Approach

Round the north end of the island, and enter the harbor channel. The channel through the coral is buoyed. Le Caudan has a small basin, and yachts are moored alongside the wall.

At the Marina

Le Caudan Marina is in the capital city of Port Louis, so all services are available and convenient.

Shoreside Services

Market

The market is an easy walk through the north underpass and has fruit, vegetables, meat, fish, and a craft area upstairs.

Supermarkets

There is a nearby Winners on President Kennedy Street, behind the Air Mauritius building.

Further afield, at Bagatelle Mall, there is an excellent Food Lovers market.

Restaurants

The waterfront has a good selection of restaurants. Also, there are many restaurants at Bagatelle Mall.

Shopping

Le Caudan Waterfront has a sophisticated shopping area.

Bagatelle Mall is a very large mall with a huge variety of goods.

Telephones

You will need a local SIM card.

Water Taxi

A free water taxi operates from the marina to Le Suffren Hotel.

Taxis

Taxis are easy to hail on the street and in front of the nearby hotels.

Airport and Airlines

Sir Seewoosagur International Airport is about 25 miles from Port Louis.

Airlines include British Airways, Cathay Pacific, Air Madagascar, and Dragonair, which have offices at Le Caudan Waterfront. Also Air Mauritius and Air France have offices on Kennedy Street.

Accommodations

The Labourdonnais Waterfront Hotel is a beautiful hotel next to the dock.

Le Suffren Hotel across the waterway (free water taxi) is slightly less expensive than Labourdonnais.

Things to Do and See

Dodo Spotting (?)

To see a stuffed dodo, visit the Natural History Museum in Port Louis.

Diving

Wonderful scuba diving is available.

Tea Plantations

We rented a car to drive to lovely Cheri Bois tea plantation for a stylish lunch. There are a several tea plantations to choose from, ranging from historical to more modern.

Labourdonnais Plantation

This beautifully restored French mansion is part of a sugar plantation.

Botanical Gardens

The Pamplemousses Botanical Gardens is one of the oldest botanical gardens in the world.

National Park Gorges

Along the Riviera Noire, the gorges are stunning.

The interior of Mauritius offers lush moutains and wonderful hiking. Photo by Clément Larher (License CC BY-SA 3.0).

Data SIO, NOAA, U.S. Navy, NGA, GEBCO
Image Landsat
Image IBCAO

N

Passage Notes
(Mauritius to La Réunion)

- **QuickFacts**
  — Mileage: 132 nm
  — Duration: One overnight
  — Dates: October 23, 2014–October 24, 2014

Expected Conditions

This is a brief, overnight passage that you can time to conducive weather. Nonetheless, as the Indian Ocean current splits to go around Mauritius, there is an area of turbulence on the west side of the island where the current rejoins itself. This can cause an hour or two of washing-machine conditions regardless of the surrounding conditions.

Places We Visited along the Way

None.

Other Possible Stops

None suggested.

Arrival

We were welcomed on arrival on October 24, 2014, and had cocktails and dinner at the marina's Dodo Restaurant.

1. Marina with fuel dock and marine services
2. New marina under construction
3. Downtown Le Port

In Brief

La Réunion is a department of France and is the last volcanic island in this chain.

Website

www.la-reunion-tourisme.com

Customs and Immigration

As a department of France, the entry requirements are identical to a visit to Europe.

Visas

Not normally required.

La Réunion Island

(Port of Entry)

Le Port Harbor

Coordinates: 20°56′ S, 55°16′ E

Charts: BA 1495

Guides: *Ocean Passages & Landfalls* (Heikell and O'Grady)
Indian Ocean Cruising Guide (Heikell)

- ## QuickFacts
  — Time: UTC + 4
  — Language: French (and English for most tourist activities)
  — Currency: Euro
  — Weather/Climate: Tropical
  — Tides/Current: Insignificant
  — Fuel: A fuel dock is located at the end of the seawall
  — Power: 250V 50Hz
  — Water: Potable water on the dock

Approach

You should round the island to the north and enter the harbor from the west. Then a U-turn to starboard to round the rocks at the end of the seawall will put you in the small-boat marina. Tie up to the seawall, where you can reach a ladder to climb out.

A large marina with floating docks is under construction.

At the Marina

Le Port is about 10 miles from the capital city of St. Denis. This is a great location from which to explore the island.

There are several boat-related shops and repair facilities on the dock.

Shoreside Services

Market

There is a fresh produce market in Le Port, about a 20-minute walk.

Supermarkets

Both Leader Price and Jumbo are a short taxi ride (or a long walk) away.

Restaurants

The Dodo Restaurant is at the marina, and there is a good selection in Le Port.

Shopping

There are a variety of stores in Le Port.

There are several chandleries on the dock. They have services and stock for most repairs and can arrange for parts to be imported as well.

Telephone

A local SIM card should provide good service.

Taxis

The nearby petrol station has a van/taxi, and taxis can be arranged by phone.

Airport and Airlines

The airport is Roland Garros International with flights to South Africa and Europe via major airlines, such as Air France.

Accommodations

There is a good selection of nearby hotels.

Things to Do and See

Tourist Office/Office de Tourisme

They can arrange diving, renting a car or jeep, mountain climbing, or visiting the steaming volcano.

Helicopter Tour of the Island

We took a breathtaking flight using the Heliagon Company and toured Le Lagon, Le Dimitile Mafate, Plaine des Sables, La Fournaise, Trou de fer Salazie, and Cilaos. It was an amazing ride!

One of the many stunning waterfalls we saw from our helicopter tour which also make for a great hike.

Piton De La Fournaise is the largest volcano on the island, and it began erupting again in August 2015. Photo by Sebastian Appelt (License CC BY-SA 4.0).

Passage Notes

(La Réunion to Richards Bay, South Africa)

Expected Conditions

This may have been the roughest passage of the entire circumnavigation. Depressions come up out of the Antarctic on a regular basis and disrupt the trade winds. Unfortunately, this passage is long enough to extend beyond the limit of accurate forecasting, so there is no way to ensure favorable conditions for the entire passage.

Accordingly, start out with the best conditions you can foresee and ride out whatever you encounter.

About 50 miles off the South African coast, you'll encounter the south-flowing Agulhas Current, which flows down the African coast at up to 5 knots. This is the equivalent in many ways of Florida's Gulf Stream in that it is warm water and in that it can be dangerous in conditions where wind opposes the current.

If you have trade wind conditions, the current is no problem (except you need to plan for the set). Low pressure systems come up from the south every week or so. If you encounter one and the wind is southerly, depending on its strength, it may be preferable to stand off outside the current until the wind rounds more favorably.

Caution: Give a wide berth of 80-plus nm to Madagascar for two reasons: first, the water is shallow, and if you are caught there when a low rolls through, it can become very rough, and second, there have been incidents of piracy along the coast.

QuickFacts
— Mileage: 1,380 nm
— Duration: Eight days
— Dates: October 31, 2014–November 8, 2014

Places We Visited along the Way
None.

Other Possible Stops

Madagascar
Some cruisers visit Madagascar, but we do not recommend it, as the only harbor is well off the direct route and political instability and piracy make a visit risky.

Arrival
South Africa at last! A very nice greeting at the Zululand Yacht Club on November 8, 2014.

S/V *Celebrate* Blog: Heading for Durban

November 12, 2014

Our stay at Richards Bay has been great, with a first-class welcome from the Zululand Yacht Club. Len, one of their rear commodores, and Joel from World Cruising Club have worked their socks off to help the fleet in at all times of the day and night. Also, the presentation of a bottle of local bubbly and a club burgee made it one of the best landfalls on the trip. Just before getting in, we also had a welcoming committee in the form of a humpback whale that breached about a mile away from us, followed by two babies.

The Zululand Yacht Club has lots of character (a proper yacht club) and was just the place to conclude a bumpy passage. All the fleet have now arrived and are making a start on repairs and plans to explore. We have also met lots of characters over a drink (or two) in the bar and at the Braai (BBQ in English). Liz, the club secretary, originally from Ireland, was a treasure, particularly when she and Derry and Margaret from Avocet, our very own Irish ambassadors, were singing Irish anthems to celebrate their victory over South Africa in rugby.

In our short stay, we have also seen some of the wildlife; yesterday a World ARC tour took us to Hulhluwe Game Reserve. We saw many elephants, at one point counting a herd of 17, white rhinos, giraffes, zebras, buffalo, warthogs, and lesser-known nyala (like an antelope). The lions and leopards did not want to come out to see us, so, sadly, we cannot claim the big five yet (lion, leopard, buffalo, rhino, and elephant).

(To read the complete blogs, go to worldsailing.guru/blogs.)

SOUTH AFRICA

(November 8, 2014–January 10, 2015)

Photo by Kevin Pluck (License CC BY 2.0).

- Zululand Yacht Club Marina (Richards Bay)
- Victoria and Alfred (V&A) Marina (Cape Town, Cape of Good Hope)

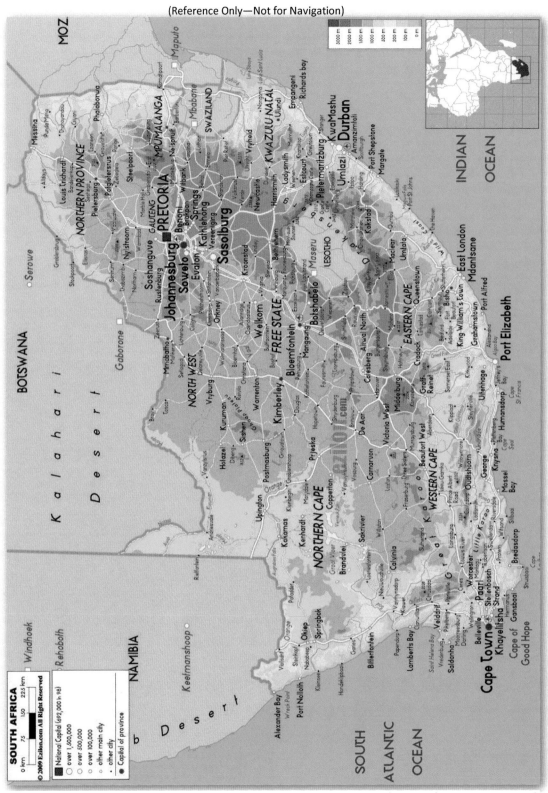

(Reference Only—Not for Navigation)

From Vidiani.com (License CC BY-SA 4.0).

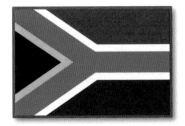

SOUTH AFRICA

Coordinates: 28°47' S, 32°04' E
(Richards Bay)
Charts: BA 4173, BA 4174, BA 4148, BA 1846
Guides: *Ocean Passages & Landfalls* (Heikell and O'Grady)
South African Almanac (Morgan)

In Brief

South Africa spans the southern tip of the African continent with shores on both the Atlantic and Indian Oceans. Although many people believe the Cape of Good Hope is the southernmost point, sailors learn that the tip is actually Cape Agulhas, and the Cape of Good Hope is actually nearly a hundred miles to the northwest.

Website

www.southafrica.net

Customs and Immigration

There is plenty of paperwork to do. To complicate matters, you'll need to check into and check out from (and file a "flight" plan with) every South African port you visit.

On arrival, you may be directed to a customs dock for clearance, or you may be able to check in from your marina.

▪ QuickFacts

— Time: UTC+2
— Language: English, Afrikaans
— Currency: Rand
— Weather/Climate: Subtropical
— Tides/Currents: Currents are strong along the east coast. Tides are generally just a few feet

Visas

You probably don't need a visa in advance to visit South Africa. To verify, check their official website:

http://www.southafrica.info/travel/documents/visas.htm

South Africa is most famous for its wildlife, and any visit should include a safari to view the animals! Photo by Tambako the Jaguar (License CC BY-ND 2.0).

1. *Zululand Yacht Club*
2. *Shops and check-in (and Tuzi Gazi Marina)*
3. *Downtown Richards Bay*

Zululand Yacht Club Marina

(Port of Entry)
Richards Bay

Coordinates: 28°47' S, 32°04' E

Charts: BA 4173, BA 4174

Guides: *Ocean Passages & Landfalls* (Heikell and O'Grady)

South African Almanac (Morgan)

- **QuickFacts**
  — Fuel: Fuel dock next to marina
  — Power: 250V 50Hz
  — Water: Potable water on the dock

In Brief

Founded in the late 1800s, the city of Richards Bay lies just north of the large natural bay (also Richards Bay) that is now a vibrant harbor.

Website

www.zyc.co.za

Approach

After entering the harbor, head north toward the marina, and be aware of floating booms projecting from shore on both sides of the channel.

At the Marina

The marina staff at the Zululand Yacht Club is very helpful to visiting sailors, and the marina is well sheltered.

Shoreside Services

Supermarkets

There is a Pic'n'Pay at the Boardwalk Mall a short ride away.

Restaurants

At the Zululand Yacht Club, there is a lovely restaurant and bar upstairs and many more around the area.

Shopping

There is a lot of shopping at the Boardwalk Mall.

Telephones

You can get a local SIM card, but to do so you need proof of "residency," which can be provided by the marina.

Taxis

Taxis can be arranged at the marina office.

Airport and Airlines

Richards Bay Airport is small, but you can catch flights to Johannesburg for connections worldwide.

Accommodations

There is a variety of motels in the area.

Things to Do and See

Tourist Office

The nearby tourist office can arrange excellent day tours.

Hulhluwe Game Reserve

On our tour, we saw herds of elephants, many white rhinos, giraffes, zebras, buffalo, and warthogs. It was a wonderful tour.

Passage Notes
(Richards Bay to Cape Town)

- **QuickFacts**
  - Mileage: 865 nm
  - Duration: 10 days (including 6 days at Durban)
  - Dates: November 12, 2014–November 22, 2014

Expected Conditions

Going down the east coast of Africa, beware of the Agulhas Current. If you have favorable winds, it will give you an excellent speed boost. If the winds are against you, the slop will range from unpleasant to extremely dangerous. For the most part, if you are caught in the current against the wind, simply heading nearer to shore will take you out of the current and into calmer conditions.

Rounding the tip of Africa at Point Agulhas, you lose the Agulhas Current and pick up the Atlantic Current coming north. The drop in water temperature is quite abrupt. We really noticed that the refrigerator and freezer suddenly became much more efficient with the colder cooling water.

On the leg north to Cape Town, be aware that an offshore wind can roar down through gaps in the coastal mountains, growing rapidly from near calm to 30-plus knots in short order.

Places We Visited along the Way

Remember, you must check out with authorities at every South African port you depart from and check back in at every port in which you arrive.

Durban

Durban is a modern city with convenient yacht services. Dock first at the customs dock and contact the marina office on VHF channel 16 for a slip assignment. The yacht clubs cooperate for visitor dockage and are conveniently located for access to the city by foot.

There is no fuel at the marina, but the marina office can arrange for a local station to bring out a tank trailer with a hose that will reach to the customs dock. All the arrival paperwork can be handled through the marina and a visit to your boat by officials. Departure, however, requires a visit to Customs and Immigration, about a 20-minute walk away.

We found it very hospitable here.

1. *Entrance channel—beware of shipping traffic*
2. *Yacht clubs and downtown Durban*

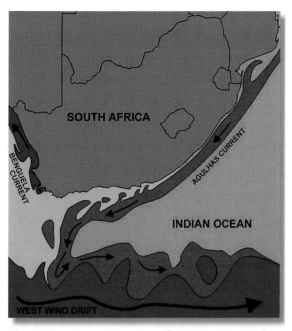

The Agulhas Current is a river of warm water that flows down the east coast of Africa, similar to the Gulf Stream flowing up the east coast of Florida. Figure by Oggmus (License CC BY-SA 4.0.

The Durban skyline. Photo by Terrence Franck (License CC BY-ND 2.0).

Other Possible Stops

Port Elizabeth—This stop is convenient for waiting for favorable weather.

Mossel Bay—This stop is convenient for fuel (we refueled here) and has both dockage and anchorage if you need to wait for favorable weather for the trip northwest to Cape Town.

False Bay—Simon's Town (no relation that we know of) has a marina that may be a convenient stop before rounding the Cape of Good Hope.

Arrival

Our first glimpse of the famous Table Mountain of Cape Town was on our arrival on November 22, 2014.

View as we arrived in Cape Town. Photo by George Groutas (License CC BY 2.0).

1. *Entry around breakwater*
2. *Swing bridge followed by bascule bridge*
3. *V&A Waterfront Marina*
4. *Customs and Immigration*
5. *Huge V&A Mall*
6. *Robben Island*

In Brief

With a fascinating history and a unique geographical position on the major trade routes, Cape Town is one of the highlights of the cruise. Also, the Victoria and Alfred (V&A) Waterfront is a massive commercial development with the marina, deluxe hotels, restaurants, and a huge shopping mall (blue roofs in the image above).

Website

www.waterfront.co.za

Customs and Immigration

Remember that in South Africa, you'll need to clear in with Customs and Immigration even though you are arriving from another South African port. Fortunately, the office is within walking distance of the marina, and a map is provided by the dockmaster.

Victoria and Alfred (V&A) Waterfront Marina

(Port of Entry)
Cape Town, Cape of Good Hope

Coordinates: 33°54' S, 18°25' E

Charts: 4148, 1846

Guides: *Ocean Passages & Landfalls* (Heikell and O'Grady)

South African Almanac (Morgan)

▪ QuickFacts

— Fuel: Potentially very rough, small fuel dock in the main harbor outside the bridges. Also available at the Royal Cape Yacht Club
— Power: 250V 50Hz
— Water: Potable water on the dock

Approach

Cape Town harbor is a major shipping port, and yachts are advised to call harbor control on VHF channel 16 before entering. Because it's a large freight harbor, Cape Town is well surveyed and marked.

The marina is obstructed by a swing bridge and then a bascule bridge, both of which open at 15 minutes before and after the hour. Happily, they are operated by the same bridgetender, so one call on VHF channel 71 is all you need for entrance.

At the Marina

A full-service marina. After settling in and exploring by foot, you'll find more in the vicinity of the marina than you can do during your stay. We were there for almost two months to coordinate with the most agreeable predicted weather patterns.

Many cruisers prefer the Royal Cape Yacht Club, about 2 miles to the southwest. It has fuel and other boat services but is beyond walking distance to most shopping, and they limit boat length to 50 feet.

Shoreside Services

Supermarkets

There is an excellent supermarket close by in the lower level of the V&A Mall. Depending on where your slip is, it's a bit of a hike with a large load of groceries, so several trips may be in order.

Celebrate is docked in front of the condos at the V&A Waterfron Marina with Table Mountain in the backgound Photo by Jay Ailworth.

Restaurants

There are many, many restaurants around the marina and in the mall.

Shopping

The huge V&A shopping complex is amazing! Also, there are other interesting shops around the marina.

For the boat: You can easily refit and repair your boat here, and we used Nautical Gods Yacht Management to find parts and excellent workers for us.

Telephones

Keep your SIM card from Richards Bay, and you'll have excellent cell phone service in Cape Town.

Taxis

Taxis are always available at the hotels surrounding the marina.

Airport and Airlines

About a half hour away, Cape Town International Airport is a modern, world-class facility with flights worldwide.

TIP: When arriving by air, note that the "limousine" service sold within the airport is a shared-ride business that might cost more and take longer than the taxis lined up outside.

Accommodations

Many luxurious hotels are on the waterfront.

Things to Do and See

Tourist Office

The tourist office is on the waterfront.

Hop-On Hop-Off Bus Tour

The bus offers several routes with a narrative that gives a great introduction to Cape Town and the local surrounding area. The main stop is right at the marina.

Aquarium

The Two-Oceans Aquarium is right on the waterfront overlooking the marina.

This is the view from the top of Table Mountain looking back at Celebrate *(center). We took the gondola up, but the more athletic can take a trail.*

Table Mountain

Go up Table Mountain for a spectacular view and lunch. You can take the hop-on bus to the tramway, or, for the more adventuresome, you can hike to the top.

Robben Island

Take a boat tour to Robben Island (where Nelson Mandela was incarcerated).

Forgotten Train (Route)

Take the Forgotten Train tour to Naroo with winery and brandy-tasting visits. The tour was a step back in time with excellent narratives on South African history.

Game Reserves

Visit a game reserve for an unforgettable wildlife experience. We flew to the wonderful Camp Jubulani Game Preserve for a safari next to Kruger National Park.

Stellenbosch (Wine Country)

The wineries in the area are stellar with amazing restaurants to match.

One of our wildlife-viewing excursions was on elephant back. A rough ride, but worth it!

Stellenbosch vineyards. Photo by HelenSTB (License CC BY-SA 2.0).

All the animals you'd expect are in the wilds.

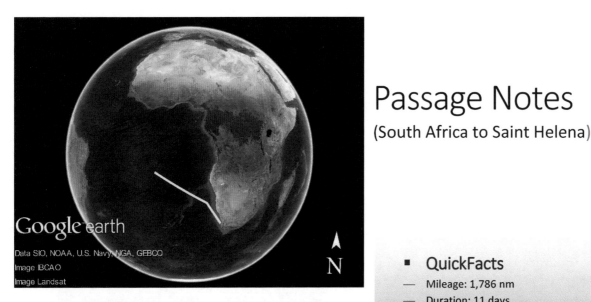

Passage Notes

(South Africa to Saint Helena)

- **QuickFacts**
  - Mileage: 1,786 nm
  - Duration: 11 days
  - Dates: January 10, 2015–January 21, 2015

Expected Conditions

After the South Atlantic storm season abates, you should expect fresh winds near Cape Town, dwindling to light to moderate further north. By staying near Africa for a few hundred miles before heading out into the Atlantic, you'll get more favorable currents to Saint Helena.

Other Possible Stops

Saldahna—60 miles north of Cape Town on the coast of South Africa.

Places We Visited along the Way

Dassen Island

We anchored here (33°24.911' S, 018°05.098' E) for an autopilot repair. It is a very pleasant anchorage with cape penguins and many birds on shore.

Arrival

At Saint Helena, we secured ourselves bow and stern between two mooring buoys as required by the port authorities.

There was a warm welcome from the yacht club on the dock.

Although Dassen Island was not in our original plans, it was comfortable and scenic. Photo by Harvey Barrison (License CC BY-SA 2.0).

S/V *Celebrate* Blog: Napoleon's Last Days, Centuries-Old Military History, and Stunning Views on Tour of Saint Helena Island in the Mid-South Atlantic Ocean

January 23, 2015

This very remote British island territory can be reached only by boat currently, but an airport is under construction. The first all-day tour stop was Napoleon's initial housing, Briars Pavilion, where he waited for permanent quarters for himself and his entourage to be completed. Briars was a charming house and gardens where he was officially a guest of the family who owned the property. Napoleon's last residence on Saint Helena, where he passed away, was Longwood House. The house contained elegant furnishings, and the garden areas were lovely. Napoleon picked the peaceful Sane Valley as his burial place. Later, the French government removed his body from the tomb for burial in Paris. The island's military history dates back to its strategic location during the British Empire. It was also used as a place of exile for many key prisoners, including the Boers. Historic fortifications with fabulous views include Ladder Hill Fort and Battery and High Knoll Fort. Other interesting sightings were the Heart-Shaped Waterfall, the governor's residence called Plantation House, and Sandy Bay, with prominent exposed spires named Lot and Lot's Wife. Also, Saint Helena is proud to be short-listed for World Heritage status.

(To read the complete blogs, go to worldsailing.guru/blogs.)

(January 21, 2015–January 24, 2015)   *Photo by Andrew Neaum (License CC BY-SA 3.0).*

- ## James Bay Anchorage/Moorage (Jamestown)

(Reference Only—Not for Navigation)

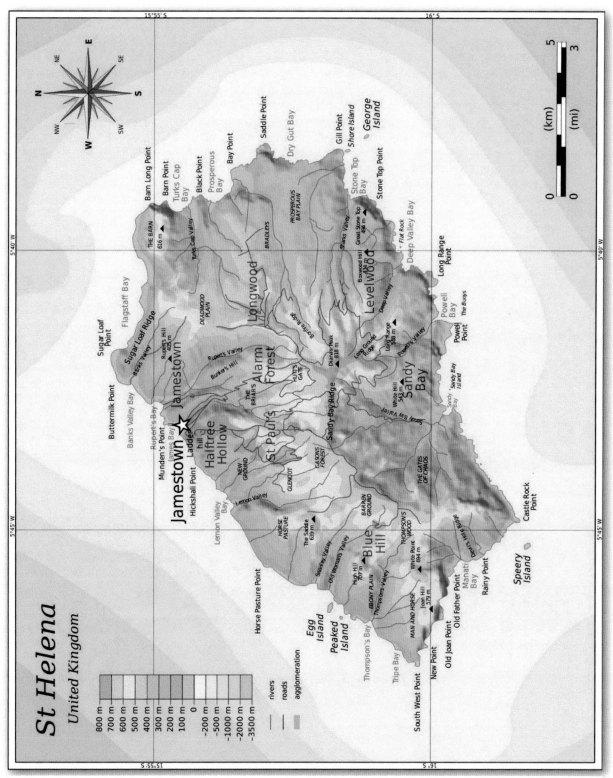

From Vidiani.com (License CC BY-SA 4.0).

QuickStart Circumnavigation Guide

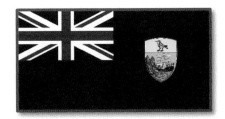

SAINT HELENA

Coordinates: 15°55' S, 05°43' W

Charts: BA 1771

Guides: *Ocean Passages & Landfalls* (Heikell and O'Grady)

South Atlantic Circuit (Morgan)

In Brief

A remote British island territory about halfway between Africa and South America in the southern Atlantic, Saint Helena (pronounced "Heleena") is a volcanic tropical island. As of this writing, it could be accessed only by boat, but a new airport is under construction.

Famously, Napoleon was exiled here until his death.

Website

www.sthelenatourism.com

Customs and Immigration

You clear in on shore. The Customs and Immigration office is at the police station, a short walk from the water-taxi

▪ QuickFacts

— Time: UTC+0
— Language: English
— Currency: Saint Helena pound
— Weather/Climate: Tropical
— Tides/Currents: Negligible

landing. Also, you must show a copy of your health insurance information.

Clearing out is the same procedure.

Jacob's Ladder descending to Jamestown. Photo by David Stanley (License CC BY 2.0).

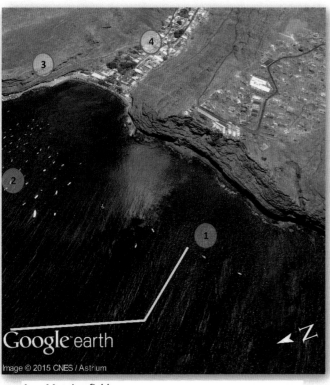

1. *Mooring field*
2. *Local craft moorings; do not enter due to many near-surface mooring lines*
3. *Water-taxi landing*
4. *Downtown Jamestown*

James Bay Anchorage/ Moorage
(Port of Entry)
Jamestown

Coordinates: 15°55' S, 05°43' W

Charts: BA 1771

Guides: *Ocean Passages & Landfalls*
(Heikell and O'Grady)
South Atlantic Circuit (Morgan)

▪ QuickFacts
— Fuel: Available for delivery to your boat
— Power: None
— Water: Watermaker operation is OK

In Brief

Historic Jamestown is Saint Helena's center of activity on this island of fewer than 5,000 inhabitants. There is a mooring field because the bottom is fairly steep-to and the anchorage is in 100-plus feet depth.

Approach

Round the island on the north, call Saint Helena Radio on VHF channel 16 when you are 10–20 miles out, and they will arrange for your buoy assignment.

At the Moorage

The buoys are quite large, and you may have to climb out on the buoy itself to tie on. Be aware that the mooring rings may chafe lines.

There is no dockage except for a temporary small boat landing and a concrete quay for ships.

Shoreside Services

Supermarkets

There is a small supermarket in town, but it is limited by Saint Helena's remoteness, and the stock varies with the arrival of the freighters.

Restaurants

At the Consulate Hotel in town, we had a great English breakfast. Also, there is a selection of cafés and pubs.

Shopping

There is a variety of small shops around town.

Telephones

There are pay phones, but there is no cell phone service on the island.

Water Taxi

There is no dinghy dock, although you may pick up and drop off at the landing, but the water taxi is very convenient.

Taxis

Taxis can be arranged at the tourist office on Main Street.

Airport and Airlines

The airport is under construction and is scheduled to open in 2016.

Accommodations

Several hotels are available.

Things to Do and See

Tourist Office

The tourist office is located on Main Street.

Jacob's Ladder

The ladder was originally a cable railway to take troops to the promontory above the town, but now the steps provide excellent exercise for the more adventuresome.

Island Tour

Our tour included a visit to Briar's Pavilion, Napoleon's initial housing on Saint Helena, followed by Longwood House, Napoleon's final home (under house arrest).

We also visited Napoleon's first tomb in the Sane Valley. Additional stops were Plantation House (the governor's residence) and the previous century's Ladder Hill Fort and High Knoll Fort. There was a heart-shaped waterfall and a visit to Sandy Bay with exposed rock spires called Lot and Lot's Wife.

Diving

This is one of the world's best opportunities to dive with whale sharks, the world's largest fish.

Diving with whale sharks is quite an adventure, although they have no teeth and are completely harmless. Photo by Marcel Ekkel (License CC BY 2.0).

Napoleon's original grave on Saint Helena is very plain relative to the grand tomb subsequently built for him in Paris. Photo by David Stanley (License CC BY 2.0).

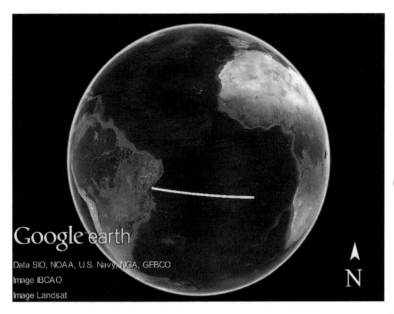

Passage Notes

(Saint Helena to Salvador, Brazil)

Expected Conditions

There was some wind along the way but also a lot of motoring.

Places We Visited along the Way

None.

Other Possible Stops

Ascension Island—Ascension is northwest of Saint Helena and can be visited if you plan to enter Brazil further north or if you are heading directly back to Europe.

Recife, Brazil—Many sailors choose to enter Brazil at Recife rather than Salvador, as we did.

QuickFacts

— Mileage: 1,951 nm
— Duration: 13 days
— Dates: January 24, 2015–February 6, 2015

Ilha Fernando de Noronha, Brazil—A beautiful nature preserve area. Not officially a port of entry to Brazil, but some cruisers have been allowed to visit prior to arriving at the mainland for official entry.

Arrival

We arrived in Salvador, Brazil, at night on February 7, 2015, and had no trouble entering the bay. We anchored temporarily on sand outside the marina to wait for daylight.

Recife Harbor. Photo by Portal da Copa/ME (License CC BY 3.0).

S/V *Celebrate* Blog: Caipirinha Cocktails, Clifftop Elevator, and a Romantic Restaurant in Salvador, Brazil

February 13, 2015

Our terrific Rally Control, Suzana, Joel, and Johnny, greeted us at the marina with caipirinha cocktails, the special beverage of Brazil, and we felt so welcomed! Just up from the marina is a huge cliff face elevator that transports you up to the old town. What a ride! Next, we ate dinner at a beautifully restored restaurant, recommended by Suzana, with wonderful food and centuries-old ambience. We left Salvador too soon but had dates to meet in Grenada.

(To read the complete blogs, go to worldsailing.guru/blogs.)

(February 6, 2015–February 10, 2015)   *Photo by Adam Jones, adamjones.freeservers.com (License CC BY-SA 3.0).*

- Terminal Nautico Da Bahia (Salvador de Bahia)

(Reference Only—Not for Navigation)

QuickStart Circumnavigation Guide

BRAZIL

Coordinates: 12°58' S, 38°30' W

Charts: BA 540, BA 545

Guides: *Ocean Passages & Landfalls* (Heikell and O'Grady)

Havens and Anchorages (Morgan)

South Atlantic Circuit (Morgan)

Brazil Cruising Guide (Balette)

In Brief

A previous Portuguese colony, Brazil has almost half the territory of South America, including the Amazon River Basin with a diversity of wildlife.

Caution: Crime is an issue, and you should be vigilant.

Website

www.Braziltour.com

Customs and Immigration

Entry by boat first requires a visit to Immigration by the skipper with all crew passports. Next, you will need to visit Customs, then the Health Department to present vaccination certificates. Finally, you will make a visit to the port captain.

▪ QuickFacts
— Time: UTC-3
— Language: Portuguese
— Currency: Real
— Weather/Climate: Tropical
— Tides/Currents: Six feet

Visas

Citizens of the United States of America must obtain a visa prior to embarking for Brazil. These can be obtained by visiting a Brazilian consulate.

Paddling in Salvador de Bahia. Photo by Clarissa Pacheco (License CC BY 2.0).

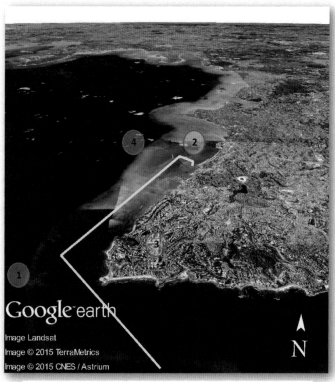

Image Landsat
Image © 2015 TerraMetrics
Image © 2015 CNES / Astrium

1. *Wide-open, well-marked entry from the South Atlantic*
2. *Terminal Nautico Marina*
3. *Downtown area of the city of Salvador*
4. *Sandbar where we anchored*

In Brief

The marina's central location offers the best access to the old town.

Website

www.salvador.info

Approach

Pass either north or south of the marked bar at the mouth of Bahia de Santo, and follow the markers into the bay.

At the Marina

Mooring is Med-style to floating docks with pickup lines. Ask for a map to Customs, Immigration, Health, and the port captain.

Shoreside Services

Markets

The city is full of stalls selling fresh produce.

Supermarkets

Take a taxi to the downtown supermarkets.

Terminal Nautico Da Bahia

(Port of Entry)
Salvador de Bahia

Coordinates: 12°58' S, 38°30' W
Charts: BA 540, BA 545
Guides: *Ocean Passages & Landfalls*
         (Heikell and O'Grady)
         Havens and Anchorages (Morgan)
         South Atlantic Circuit (Morgan)
         Brazil Cruising Guide (Balette)

Restaurants

- **QuickFacts**
  — Fuel: There is a fuel barge anchored outside the marina
  — Power: 250V 50Hz
  — Water: No potable water on the dock

Plentiful restaurants of all kinds are in the marina area.

Shopping

For the boat: there is a convenient chandlery nearby.

There are many shops and malls within walking distance.

Telephones

You can get a local SIM card at the store near the marina.

Taxis

There is a taxi stand at the exit to the marina, and taxis are plentiful.

Airport and Airlines

Deputado Luis Eduardo Magalhaes Airport is about 20 miles from town and has many flights, but you'll probably need to change planes in São Paulo or Rio.

Accommodations

There is a variety of hotels at the top of the hillside next to the top of the cliff-side elevator.

Things to Do and See

Tourist Office

At the top of the cliff elevator is Tours Bahia, a multilingual agency for arranging tours.

Cliff-Face Elevator

Take the elevator to the top of the hill. What a ride!

Salvador Cathedral

The Salvador Cathedral was built in the early 1600s and is the largest cathedral outside of Rome.

The elevator up the cliff to the old town. Photo by Jay Ailworth.

Considered the world's biggest party, Carnival is a jubilant citywide extravaganza and is the reason many visit Salvador. Photo by Antônio Cruz/ABr (Agência Brasil) (License CC BY 3.0 br).

Google earth

Data SIO, NOAA, U.S. Navy, NGA, GEBCO
Image Landsat
Image IBCAO

N

Passage Notes
(Salvador, Brazil, to Prickly Bay, Grenada)

Expected Conditions

Glorious sailing is possible after rounding the easternmost point of Brazil (near Recife).

Since the trade winds blow primarily westward, the first part of this journey will be upwind unless you wait for a window where the wind has veered to the southeast.

We went nonstop from Salvador to Grenada, about a 2,500 nm run (as recorded by the GPS). When compared with the log's recording of 2,264 nm through the water, that means that the Equatorial Current boosted us by 250 miles. During that run, we never ran less than 200 nm per day and arrived in Grenada four days ahead of our predicted time. Also, we had a 2-plus knot current with us for much of the trip.

A fascinating feature of the passage was the abrupt change in water color from blue to brown where the outflow of the Amazon River meets the Equatorial Current, even though we were over 75 nm offshore. Also, we crossed the Equator for the second time on February 17, 2015. In addition, we celebrated passing the milestone of 100,000 nm at sea.

Places We Visited along the Way

None.

Other Possible Stops

Bahia de Santos—The great bay with Salvador at its mouth is a great cruising ground.

Recife—See page 114.

- **QuickFacts**
  — Mileage: 2,264 nm
  — Duration: 13 days
  — Dates: February 10, 2015–February 23, 2015

Ilha Fernando de Noronha—See page 114.

Trinidad and Tobago—A wonderful stop at the southern end of the Caribbean cruising area. The greatest issue with the Caribbean is that there are so many wonderful places to visit that you can only scratch the surface in a single season.

Arrival

Arrival in Grenada can be painless, with a wide-open, well-marked anchorage, convenient dockage, and on-site check-in facilities. We found this at the Prickly Bay Marina/Moorage/Anchorage, where we arrived on February 23, 2014, and secured a mooring ball.

S/V *Celebrate* Blog: Great All-Day, Island-Wide Safari Tour by Henry in Grenada!

March 2, 2015

Henry's Safari Tours' Kurt, a very nice young man, picked us up at the Prickly Bay Marina, where they have a sales office, and we were joined by a lovely Norwegian couple. First stop was the beautiful Concord Waterfall, complete with a young boy who would dive from the cliff top into the pool made by the waterfall. It was jaw-dropping and we have the pictures to prove it! Continuing along the west coast with picturesque views of the beaches and sailboats going by, we stopped at Gouyave to tour a three-story nutmeg factory. The process is mostly by hand, beginning with drying the nuts on one factory level, putting them through a cracking machine on another level, and dropping them to the main floor for hand grading and shipping. A tasty buffet lunch overlooking the beach at Sauteurs Bay was next. Close by we saw the famous Caribes' Leap, where the Caribs jumped off the cliff to their death rather than surrender to the French.

On a happier note, our next visit was to the rum distillery of River Antoine. It was interesting to see the large waterwheel still in service for crushing the cane. Of course, they have gone from aging in oak barrels to processing in stainless steel vats. We had a terrific tasting of several overproof rums, their dessert cream rum, and fruit rum punch. Next, we visited the Grand Etang Lake, which is a volcanic crater lake surrounded by lush forest. Then, it was back to Prickly Bay and grilled steaks on the boat. Grenada is a wonderful place!

(To read the complete blogs, go to worldsailing.guru/blogs.)

(February 23, 2015–March 16, 2015)   *Underwater sculpture* Vicissitudes *in Moliniere Bay. Photo by Kevin (License CC BY 2.0).*

- Prickly Bay Marina/Moorage/Anchorage (Prickly Bay)

(Reference Only—Not for Navigation)

From Vidiani.com (License CC BY-SA 4.0).

QuickStart Circumnavigation Guide

GRENADA

Coordinates: 12°02' N, 61°45' W

Charts: BA 797

Guides: *Ocean Passages & Landfalls* (Heikell and O'Grady)

A Sailor's Guide to the Windward Islands (Doyle)

Grenada to the Virgin Islands (Patuelli)

In Brief

Grenada is an island country and one of the southernmost Caribbean Windward Islands. Grenada is also called the "Island of Spice" due to the large nutmeg and mace industry.

After our passage from Brazil, we wanted to spend a day or two at anchor to unwind, so we chose to enter at Prickly Bay on the south coast.

Website

www.grenadagrenadines.com

Customs and Immigration

Ports of entry include Prickly Bay and the Port Louis Marina.

▪ QuickFacts

— Time: UTC-4
— Language: English
— Currency: East Caribbean dollar (ECD)
— Weather/Climate: Tropical
— Tides/Currents: The Caribbean current and tidal flows are generally minimal, but currents concentrate in channels between islands

Visas

A visa is not needed for US citizens. For updates, visit:

www.grenadaconsulate.com/visa_exempt.htm

Looking north across Saint George's Harbor, Grenada. Photo by Ian Mackenzie (License CC BY 2.0).

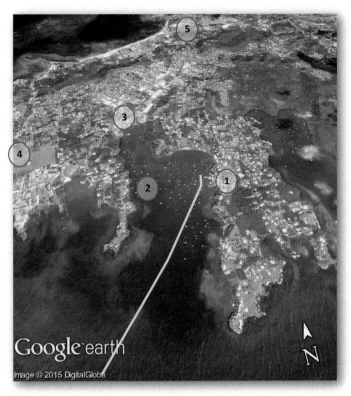

1. Prickly Bay Marina with fuel dock and check-ins
2. Mooring field and anchorage
3. Marine store and boatyard
4. Airport
5. Port Louis

Prickly Bay Marina/Moorage/ Anchorage

(Port of Entry)
Prickly Bay

Coordinates: 12°02' N, 61°45' W

Charts: BA 797

Guides: *Ocean Passages & Landfalls* (Heikell and O'Grady)
A Sailor's Guide to the Windward Islands (Doyle)
Grenada to the Virgin Islands (Patuelli)

■ **QuickFacts**

— Fuel: Fuel dock at marina
— Power: 120V 60Hz
— Water: Water on the dock and crystal-clear water for watermaker use

In Brief

This is the most popular moorage/anchorage on the south side of Grenada. Surge may make mooring/anchoring preferable to the dock.

Many cruisers go to the Port Louis Marina at Port Louis on the eastern shore.

Websites

pricklybaymarina.com

Approach

Go south of the off-lying charted shoals, and enter the bay on 30°Magnetic. Prickly Bay Marina is on the east side of the bay, and you can call them on VHF channel 16 to visit the fuel dock or arrange moorage. There is a no-anchor area to keep the marina entrance clear.

Customs and Immigration

All formalities can be completed in minutes at the office, which is conveniently located upstairs in the building behind the marina office.

At the Marina

This is a full-service, capable marina with a cheerful, helpful staff. Also, there is a small chandlery at the marina office and a large chandlery at the boatyard at the head of the bay, a few minutes away by dinghy.

Shoreside Services

Supermarkets

Groceries are at several supermarkets a reasonable taxi ride away. We went to the Spice Island Mall and had an easy time provisioning.

Restaurants

There is a pizza restaurant at the marina and a selection of restaurants at the head of the bay with wonderful dining throughout the island.

Shopping

The Grand Anse Shopping Mall has a nice variety of stores.

Telephones

You can get a local SIM card at the store at the marina. Be aware that although the same company services many Caribbean islands, SIM card time on one island may be treated as international roaming on others. Don't load up on prepaid time on one island expecting to use it as you continue north.

Taxis

The marina will be happy to call you a taxi, but a common practice is to walk to the street at the head of the bay and be picked up by one of the numerous shared vans, which cruise all the time.

Airport and Airlines

Maurice Bishop International Airport is a short taxi ride from Prickly Bay and about 15 minutes from Port Louis. It has many direct international flights.

Accommodations

A good selection of hotels is nearby.

Things to Do and See

Tourist Office

The tourist office is in town at Saint George's.

Island Tour

We used Henry's Safari Tours for our day-long island circle tour, which included the Concord Waterfall, the Gouyava Nutmeg factory, lunch at a cliff overlook at Sauteurs Bay, the famous Caribes' Leap, the River Antoine Rum Distillery, and the Grand Etang Lake.

Diving

The underwater sculptures at Moliniere Bay are a terrific snorkel or dive. There are also many other scuba trips available.

The lionfish is venomous and is an invasive species in the Caribbean. When we went diving at Carriacou Bay, there was a bounty, and we collected three. Photo by Derek Ramsey (Ram-Man) (License CC BY-SA 2.5).

There is plenty of wonderful anchorage space available on the southern coast of Grenada. Photo by Tony Hisgett (License CC BY 2.0).

Passage Notes

(Prickly Bay, Grenada, to Rodney Bay, Saint Lucia)

- **QuickFacts**
  — Mileage: 144 nm
  — Duration: 48 days (including 36 days in True Blue, Grand Mal, Happy Hill, Carriacou, and Marigot Bay
  — Dates: February 23, 2015–April 11, 2015

Expected Conditions

We cruised leisurely up the west coast of Grenada and up to Saint Lucia. Sailing up the lee side of the island chain, be prepared for light winds near islands and sudden, much heavier winds through the gaps between them.

Places We Visited along the Way

You're back in the Caribbean now, so the possibilities here are endless.

True Blue Bay

We anchored at 12°02.179' N, 61°45.454' W. There is a great restaurant ashore.

Grand Mal Bay

We anchored off Grand Anse Beach at 12°05.601' N, 61°45.449' W. The beach is excellent.

Happy Hill (Flamingo Bay)

We picked up a mooring buoy, as is required in many of Grenada's protected waters. Then we took a terrific snorkeling trip to the underwater sculpture garden in adjacent Moliniere Bay.

Carriacou Island (Part of Grenada)

This is a port of entry for Grenada and is the last opportunity for a northbound vessel to check out of the country. The boatyard in the main anchorage in Tyrell Bay is the new location for customs and immigration.

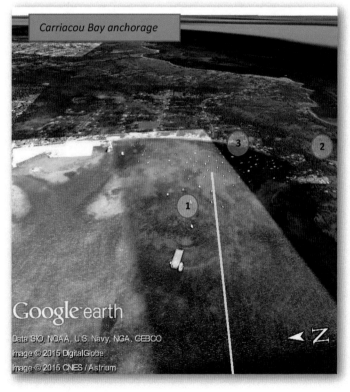

Carriacou Bay anchorage

1. Anchorage area
2. Boatyard and check-ins/checkouts
3. Beachside shops and restaurants

Marigot Bay

Rather than going directly to Rodney Bay, we went to Marigot Bay, which is also a Saint Lucia port of entry with a wonderful resort with a marina and moorings. There are nice restaurants and all the check-in services at the dock.

We spent a few weeks just enjoying Saint Lucia and beginning to think about this book

Some Possible Stops

Port Louis—This is a fine marina with convenient services, but we were ready to stay anchored out.

St. Vincent and the Grenadines—There are many available stops, but the Grenadines are a separate country from Grenada, so be sure to complete your entry paperwork properly.

Arrival

We arrived in Rodney Bay very happy on our "Parade of Sail" victory lap on April 11, 2015! We were planning many more celebrations on *Celebrate* for the completion of our world circumnavigation!

After 26,000 miles, we arrived once again in Rodney Bay! Photo by Jonathan Crowe, S/V Merlyn of Poole.

QuickStart Circumnavigation Guide

S/V *Celebrate* Blog: "Parade of Sail" Victory Lap, Super Pool Party, and Fabulous Dinner Party for Our "Finale" Day of Circumnavigation and Heartfelt Thanks to All!

April 13, 2015

Our "Parade of Sail" Victory Lap was a marvelous chance to see all of the other boats beautifully dressed overall with sails up and perfect for taking photos (we have one of each boat)! After arriving where we had started 15 months ago, at Rodney Bay Marina, Saint Lucia, awaiting us was a super pool party with a steel band and a fabulous dinner party with two bands in tribute for our completed circumnavigation. What an awesome finale!

Charlie and I will always feel grateful that we were so lucky to be on the best circumnavigation rally, supported by wonderfully experienced and gracious staff, accompanied by stunning sailors, and sent off by fantastic friends! Enormous thanks to everyone for the encouragement you have added to our lives. First, all thanks to the World ARC, without whom we would not have had this grand adventure: Andrew Bishop, Paul Tetlow, Suzana Buraca, Joel Chadwick, Chris Tibbs, Davide Sini, Hugh Murray-Walker, Rob Gaffney, Johny Buraca, and the World Cruising Club office staff. Next, appreciation to our amazing friends who were standing at S/V *Celebrate* with fresh food to add to our stock as we left the dock in Saint Lucia: Stacey and Anne Cowles, Dr. David and Rebecca Egger, Don and Charlotte Lamp, and Dr. John and Priscilla Cadwell. Also, special friends John and Kat Langenheim were waiting for us with many goodies and to join us for the Panama Canal transit. Then, to our excellent crew, we would love to have you aboard again: Andy Barrow (Puerto Vallarta, Mexico), Randy Brand (Fairbanks, Alaska), Peter Sandover (Devon, United Kingdom), and Jay Ailworth (Jupiter, Florida). Lastly, so many, many thanks needed for the wonderful sailors and boats who helped everyone in so many ways for a year and a half! We will miss you! Congratulations, everybody!

(To read the complete blogs, go to worldsailing.guru/blogs.)

(March 17, 2015–April 13, 2015)   *The World ARC fleet arrives at Marigot Bay. Photo by World ARC.*

- Rodney Bay Marina (Castries)

(Reference Only—Not for Navigation)

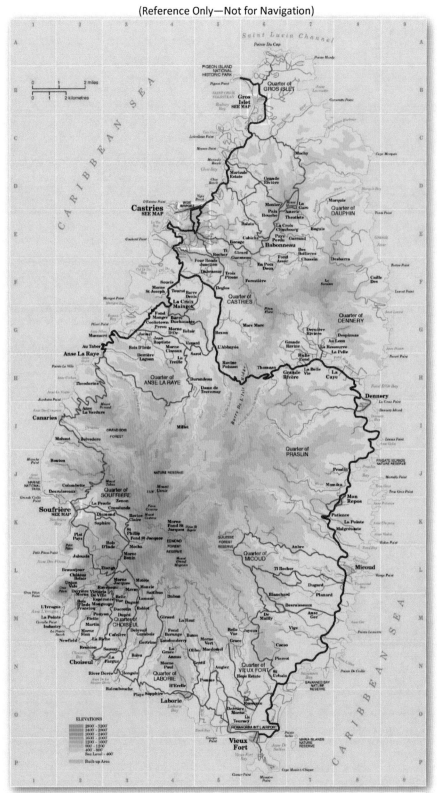

From Vidiani.com (License CC BY-SA 4.0).

SAINT LUCIA

Coordinates: 14°04' N, 060°57' W (Rodney Bay)

Charts: BA 1273

Guides: *Ocean Passages & Landfalls* (Heikell and O'Grady)

A Sailor's Guide to the Windward Islands (Doyle)

Grenada to the Virgin Islands (Patuelli)

In Brief

Saint Lucia is an independent island country in the Caribbean, West Indies, and part of the Lesser Antilles and the Windward Islands.

Website

www.stlucia.org

Customs and Immigration

Customs and Immigration is moving to online form submission, which will speed check-in and checkout procedures. Offices are located in both the Rodney Bay Marina and the Marigot Bay Marina. Go to your slip first, and then walk up to the offices.

- ## ▪ QuickFacts
  - — Time: UTC-4
  - — Language: English
  - — Currency: East Caribbean dollar
  - — Weather/Climate: Tropical
  - — Tides/Currents: One-foot tidal range—current between islands can be significant

At the southern end of Saint Lucia are active volcanos, including Gros Piton. Photo by Jean-Marc Astesana (License CC BY-SA 2.0).

1. *Rodney Bay Marina with check-ins and shops*
2. *Boatyard and fuel dock*
3. *Beachside resorts*

Rodney Bay Marina
(Port of Entry)
Castries

Coordinates: 14°04' N, 60°57' W

Charts: BA 1273

Guides: *Ocean Passages & Landfalls*
(Heikell and O'Grady)
A Sailor's Guide to the Windward Islands (Doyle)
Grenada to the Virgin Islands (Patuelli)

- ## QuickFacts
  — Fuel: Fuel dock next to marina
  — Power: Both 250V 50Hz and 120V 60Hz
  — Water: Potable water on the dock

In Brief

Rodney Bay is a large bay along the northwest coast of the island of Saint Lucia with a major anchorage area and the huge marina complex nestled in the inner harbor.

Website

www.igy-rodneybay.com

Approach

The entrance is straightforward, although the entrance channel is narrow and has a lot of small-boat traffic. You can hail the marina on VHF channel 16.

At the Marina

The marina is complete with a pool and numerous on-site restaurants, activities, and a small set of shops.

With a chandlery on-site, a hardware store across the street, and a boatyard with haul-out facilities at the north end of the marina, all boat services can be done.

Shoreside Services

Market

From the flag-flying dinghy, Gregory has a good selection of fruits and vegetables he brings to boats.

Supermarkets

Glace is a small supermarket in the marina A larger supermarket is nearby by taxi or dinghy near the JQ Mall, which has its own small dinghy dock.

Restaurants

Many cafés and bars are on the marina waterfront and further afield.

Shopping

The JQ Mall has a nice variety of stores.

Telephones

You can get a local SIM card at the marina store.

Water Taxis

These will take you to the beach and other parts of the island.

Taxis

Taxis are always available at the entry to the marina, and prices are regulated.

Airport and Airlines

Hewanorra International Airport is at the southern tip of Saint Lucia and is about 90 minutes away by taxi. The airport has direct service by British Airways, Virgin Airlines, and Air France.

Accommodations

There are many luxury hotels and resorts around the bay.

Ocean view out from the Fond Doux. Photo by jplahm (License CC BY-ND 2.0).

Steaming sulfur pits in the Caribbean's only drive-through volcano, near Soufriere. Photo by Mary-Lynn (License CC BY 2.0).

Things to Do and See

Island Tour

By boat or car, tours can be arranged at the top of the dock. We took an all-day island tour by car, stopping for a jelly (drinking coconut) along the way. At the community of Soufriere (French for "Sulfur"), we toured the magnificent tropical Diamond Botanical Gardens with a wonderful golden, earth-colored waterfall. Also, the Caribbean's only drive-in volcano is one of the sites we visited. It includes mineral baths and the sulfur hot springs that give Soufriere its name. Next, we had lunch at the lovely Fond Doux Estate. To finish the day, we stopped for just-baked bread coming out of a huge clay oven. It was a great trip!

A view of the wonderful earth-colored waterfall at Diamond Botanical Gardens, Saint Lucia. Photo by Charles Hoffman (License CC BY-SA 2.0).

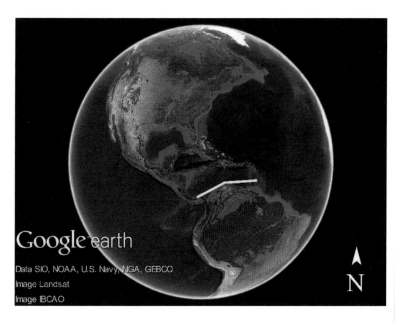

Data SIO, NOAA, U.S. Navy, NGA, GEBCO
Image Landsat
Image IBCAO

Passage Notes

(Saint Lucia to Shelter Bay Marina, Panama)

- ## QuickFacts
  - Mileage: 1,133 nm
  - Duration: 11 days (including 5 days in the San Blas Islands and Isla Linton)
  - Dates: January 11, 2014–January 22, 2014

Expected Conditions

We had strong trade-wind sailing with a few squalls. This can be a very fast passage.

Places We Visited along the Way

San Blas Islands

These are worth a trip in themselves. We spent six weeks in the San Blas Islands on a previous cruise. With the Bauhaus guide in hand, you can visit many beautiful, uninhabited islands, visit the island villages of the Kuna (Guna) Indians, or just relax in the crystal-clear waters. Many people consider the islands to be the epitome of cruising and return year after year.

At El Porvenir, we anchored at 9°33.232′ N, 78°56.915′ W. On this visit we also anchored at Chichime and West Limón Cay. El Porvenir is a port of entry to Panama, although it is not always staffed.

Isla Linton

This is a nice stop between the San Blas Islands and Shelter Bay Marina. Stopping here lets you avoid overnight passages along the way. We anchored at 9°35.652′ N, 79°35.233′ W. There is a wonderful dinghy route through the mangroves to a fine restaurant at Panamarina.

Portobello

There is an excellent anchorage at the historic Spanish port city. This bay was used by the conquistadors to load their ships with gold that had been brought across the Isthmus of Panama on burro trains, and you can visit the fortifications.

Other Possible Stops

With the excellent cruising available in the southern Caribbean, there are numerous stops you might choose. Two of the most popular are:

Aruba—This former Dutch colony is a desert island off the coast of Venezuela.

Cartagena, Colombia—With a big bay, this has become a popular stop.

Arrival

If you arrive in the San Blas Islands, Panama's entry formalities can be done at the Island of El Porvenir or, later, at Shelter Bay Marina.

The Kuna Indians of the San Blas Islands came out to our boat in their dugout canoe to sell molas. Others brought fruit, and several brought lobster, large crabs, conch, and other seafood.

Itinerary Sample

This chart shows the major ports we visited and the distance and time it took to get from one to the next. This information (in combination with port services on the next page) can be useful in planning for provisioning and considering your boat's fuel capacity. All mileages are based on our log, so they are "over water" rather than "over ground." This is the more useful number for planning and provisioning, as you can divide by your predicted boat speed and predict a passage time. With the current boost, you'll usually cover somewhat more ground.

Port	Arrival	Departure	Miles to Next Port	Days Underway	Days in Port
Shelter Bay, Panama	January 22, 2014	January 28, 2014	47	2	4
La Playita, Panama	January 29, 2014	February 5, 2014	788	5	9
San Cristobal, Galápagos	February 12, 2014	February 18, 2014	44	1	6
Santa Cruz, Galápagos	February 18, 2014	March 4, 2014	3352	22	14
Hiva Oa, French Polynesia	March 26, 2014	March 28, 2014	84	2	4
Nuku Hiva, French Polynesia	April 1, 2014	April 3, 2014	759	5	3
Papeete, French Polynesia	April 8, 2014	April 26, 2014	167	2	33
Bora Bora, French Polynesia	May 4, 2014	May 11, 2014	1325	9	7
Niue	May 20, 2014	May 24, 2014	814	6	4
Port Denarau, Fiji	May 30, 2014	June 17, 2014	16	1	19
Musket Cove, Fiji	June 17, 2014	July 4, 2014	488	3	17
Port Resolution, Vanuatu	July 7, 2014	July 10, 2014	142	1	3
Port Vila, Vanuatu	July 11, 2014	July 17, 2014	1202	6	6
Mackay, Australia	July 23, 2014	August 16, 2014	1565	9	24
Darwin, Australia	August 25, 2014	September 2, 2014	925	6	8
Bali, Indonesia	September 8, 2014	September 14, 2014	1029	6	6
Cocos (Keeling), Australia	September 20, 2014	September 29, 2014	2377	13	9
Mauritius	October 12, 2014	October 23, 2014	132	1	11
La Réunion	October 24, 2014	October 31, 2014	1380	8	7
Richards Bay, South Africa	November 8, 2014	November 12, 2014	862	4	10
Cape Town, South Africa	November 22, 2014	January 10, 2015	1786	11	49
Saint Helena	January 21, 2015	January 24, 2015	1951	13	3
Salvador, Brazil	February 6, 2015	February 10, 2015	2264	13	4
Grenada	February 23, 2015	March 16, 2015	144	4	42
Saint Lucia	April 11, 2015	January 11, 2014	1133	6	5
Panama (completing the loop)					
Total:			24776	159	307

Port Services Summary

We created this table to help us decide on provisioning and fuel planning. For example, even when fuel will be available, you may wish to overstock if your next port will require loading fuel into jerry cans and carrying it by dinghy from the beach.

	Dock/Mooring/Anchor	Electricity	Fuel	Water	Dinghy Landing	Groceries	Restaurants	Laundry	Propane	Wi-Fi	Toilets / Showers
Shelter Bay Marina, Panama	D	120/60	Barge	Y	None	Y	Dock	Y	Y	Y	
La Playita Marina, Panama	DA	120/60	Dock	Y	Dock	Y+	Nearby	Y	Y	Y	
Wreck Bay, Galápagos	A	N/A	Cans		Taxi	Y	Nearby	Y			
Academy Bay, Galápagos	A	N/A	Cans[1]		Taxi	Y	Nearby	Y			
Taaoa Bay, Hiva Oa, FP	A	N/A	Cans		Dock[2]	Y	Nearby				
Taiohae Bay, Nuku Hiva, FP	A	N/A	Dock[3]		Ladder	Y	Dock				
Marina Taina, Tahiti, FP	D	220/50	Dock	Y	N/A	Y+	Dock	Y	Y	Y	
Makai Marina, Bora Bora, FP	DM	220/50	Dock		Dock	Y	Dock	Y			
Alofi Moorage, Niue	M	N/A	None		Dock[4]	Y	Nearby	Y			
Port Denarau Marina, Fiji	DMA	220/50	Dock[5]		Dock	Y	Dock	Y	Y		
Musket Cove Marina, Fiji	DMA	220/50	Dock[6]		Dock	Y	Nearby	Y			
Port Resolution, Tanna, Vanuatu	A	N/A	None		Beach		None				
Yacht World Marina, Vanuatu	DM	220/50	Dock	Y	Dock	Y	Dock	Y			
Mackay Marina, Australia	D	220/50	Dock	Y	N/A	Y+	Dock	Y	Y		Y
Tipperary Waters Marina, Darwin, Australia	DA	220/50	Dock[7]	Y	None	Y+	Dock	Y	Y	Y	Y
Bali International Marina, Bali	D	220/50	Barge		N/A	Y	Dock	Y	Y	Y	Y
Port Refuge, Cocos (Keeling)	A	N/A	Cans		Beach	Y	Distant	Y			
Le Caudan Marina, Mauritius	D	220/50	Truck	Y	N/A	Y+	Nearby	Y			
Le Port, La Réunion	D	220/50	Dock		N/A	Y	Nearby	Y			
Zululand YC, Richards Bay, South Africa	D	220/50	Cans	Y	N/A	Y	Dock	Y	Y	Y	
V&A Waterfront Marina, Cape Town, South Africa	D	220/50	Dock[8]	Y	N/A	Y+	Nearby	Y	Y		Y
James Bay Moorage, Saint Helena	M	N/A	Delvd[9]	N	Taxi	Y	Nearby	Y	Y		Y
Terminal Nautico, Salvador, Brazil	DA	120/60	Barge	N	N/A	Y	Nearby	Y	Y	Y	Y
Prickly Bay Marina, Grenada	DMA	120/60	Dock		Dock	Y+	Dock	Y	Y	Y	Y
Rodney Bay Marina, Saint Lucia	DA	120/60 220/50	Dock		Dock	Y+	Dock	Y	Y		

Notes:

In the "Groceries" column, Y+ means US-style supermarket with consistent stock.

The "Wi-Fi" column indicates that Wi-Fi is available at the boat. Wi-Fi is available ashore everywhere except Tanna.

---

1. Enterprising local boats with large containers will deliver fuel to your boat.
2. Rough concrete.
3. Can be rough.
4. Crane to hoist dinghy.
5. Small.
6. Draft limited.
7. At different marina.
8. Can be rough.
9. The water taxi can bring out a 100-gallon container and transfer pump.

QuickStart Circumnavigation Guide

Blue-Water Passage Preparations, or How to Sail off the Edge of the World!

First Major Blue-Water Passage

It felt like sailing off the edge of the world on our first major ocean passage, around the Pinnacle Rocks of Cape Flattery at Neah Bay, in the Strait of Juan de Fuca. This was a coastal trip from Seattle to San Francisco with a few stops along the

The Pinnacles at Cape Flattery—like sailing off the edge of the world! Photo by NOAA.

way. We'd read the guides, so we knew that during a severe storm, the coast guard closes the intervening harbors, and the first all-weather entrance south of Seattle was San Francisco, about 800 miles away. Our passage turned out just fine, and we were fortunate to have enjoyable conditions most of the way.

Since then, we have accumulated over 100,000 sea miles during our world circumnavigation, several trips to Alaska, three times through the Panama Canal, and our shakedown cruise up to Nova Scotia, Canada. Along the way, Charlie earned a USCG master's license, Cathy a captain's certificate, and we read thousands of pages of cruising guides and met many other blue-water cruisers, encountering lots of useful (but sometimes conflicting) information.

We've had a chance to learn so much about blue-water passage making and hope that this digest of years of information, concentrated into a few pages, can act as a framework to help you get started on your own voyage.

If you are an experienced sailor considering your first blue-water passage or a circumnavigation, where do you start? This chapter is intended to make it easier for you, not with specific lists of "must-have" items, but with the concepts

behind them, so you can make your own decisions. We've met bay sailors on their first passage who just load up on extra provisions and cast off. At the other end of the spectrum, we've met sailors so caught up in preparations that they end up never leaving the dock. The ideas below will put you in between so you can set out with more confidence.

The priorities for any blue-water cruise are to make your trip as safe and comfortable as possible. This chapter explains how a blue-water passage is different from an afternoon on the bay and how you can prepare yourself, your crew, and your boat to have a great time on passage.

Passages Are Longer

Many people consider this idea, and many do not really get past it.

Food Storage—Obviously, if you are planning a long passage, you need food and water sufficient for the entire crew for the entire passage with some additional safety margin. You'll need a meal plan that considers the storage and refrigeration available on your boat. For a longer trip, you'll need to take into consideration that food might not be available at some of your destinations, particularly if some of your crew have special dietary needs.

On our recent world circumnavigation on *Celebrate*, we had an excellent, roomy freezer, so we could plan to have fresh fruits and vegetables for about a week out of port and then

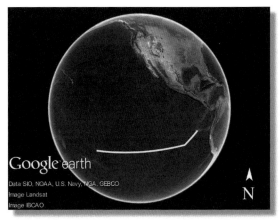

At about 3,000 miles, Galápagos to Marquesas is one of the world's longest passages without any possible intervening stops.

fall back to frozen for the duration of the passage. Because of our watch system (more about this later), we could all be together for dinner and often lunch, but everyone was on their own for breakfast and snacks, which could be taken from a large designated supply.

Fresh Water—A critical resource at sea is fresh water, and most long-distance cruisers have a watermaker on board. While it is possible to rely on shoreside water taken in tanks if you don't have a watermaker, the careful rationing and saltwater washing entailed can be a deterrent to many cruisers. But even with a watermaker, care is required. On *Celebrate*, we have a 150-gallon freshwater tank. When the gauge reached about half full, we would run the watermaker and refill it. That way, if/when the watermaker failed, we would still have 75 gallons on board, which could get us to our destination safely. We also have a saltwater foot pump at the galley sink to make it easier to get seawater when needed.

Our watermaker runs on 120V, which means it will only run when the generator (genset) is running. On our previous boat, we had a watermaker that ran on 12V, so it would run on batteries. From a practical viewpoint, even the most efficient watermaker is likely to exceed the output of your solar or other auxiliary power source, so you'll need to run your engine or genset anyway to make up the loss. This also means that even with an efficient 12V watermaker, you will need to ration water if the primary charging system fails (engine or genset), as you'll have to cut back on watermaker use.

Another point on water: Not all of your destinations will have water available. When you are at anchor in the crystal-clear waters of the Caribbean or Fiji, for example, you can run your watermaker. When you are docked in Bali, on the other hand, the water on the dock is not potable, and the water in the harbor is too dirty for watermaker operations. Although you can always purchase containers of drinking water, this led to the interesting turnabout where we had plenty of water when we were at sea but had to be much more careful when docked.

Fuel—When the wind dies, you'll probably be happy to have an engine to continue your passage. Diesel fuel is available around the world at virtually every developed destination so you can get refills, but you need to consider the fuel prospects for a passage exceeding 2,000 miles. Further, with downwind sailing, a nice 10-knot breeze, which would be fine on a reach, is insufficient to make much progress on a run, so you might be using your engine more than you expect. It's important to know how much fuel your engine uses, and you'll need to consider augmenting your boat's fuel capacity.

On *Celebrate*, we measured our fuel usage and calculated an overall range of 900 nm at 2,000 rpm. Subsequently, on our passage to the Marquesas from Galápagos (2,980 nm), we had no wind for about a week, followed by a week of great wind (but only when holding a course 10 degrees south of our destination), so when the wind died again, we had less than half our fuel remaining and still 600 miles to go to Hiva Oa. Furthermore, at Hiva Oa, fuel is available only via jerry cans, which is not really practical for the amounts of fuel needed to motor a boat the size of *Celebrate*. That's when we experimented and learned that at 1,200 rpm, the boat would make 4.5 knots and burn less than a gallon an hour. On this "restricted" fuel use, the overall range of the boat under power is actually 1,800 nm.

There are only a few really long passages in a circumnavigation, and *Celebrate*'s nearly 300-gallon fuel capacity is perfectly adequate with proper management. For most cruisers, augmenting your boat's fuel capacity with jerry cans on deck is a viable option. Many cruisers with catamarans opt for a fuel bladder in the cockpit. Transferring fuel into the main tanks can be a bit of a chore, especially when it's rough, but will usually only be necessary on the longer, windless passages.

On our previous boat, *Chére*, before we headed from Seattle through Panama to the East Coast, we added a watermaker and then converted one of the water tanks to fuel by putting in a bladder and a transfer pump. This increased the fuel capacity from 40 gallons to nearly 100 and made the trip practical.

Compare the USCG-approved flare (left) and SOLAS-approved flare (right). If you really need a flare, you'll wish you had SOLAS. Pack sturdy gloves and safety goggles with your flares; all flares are extremely hot. Photo from a video by SailingWithKids. You can see the complete video here: https://www.youtube.com/watch?v=EwNzwLTycn8.

Further from Shore

When embarking on any blue-water passage, you need to consider the ramifications of being far away from shore. Many of the priorities and techniques of sailing change: safety, navigation, communications, etc. Most of us were taught that the primary emergency procedure is a VHF "Mayday" call. What do you do when you're out of VHF range? How will you navigate when there are no landmarks?

Being Prepared—First and foremost, by being prepared, many issues that would be emergencies to the inexperienced will be avoided. You won't run out of fuel, food, or water because you have planned your capacities and managed them properly. If you tear a sail or break a halyard, you will just take things down, repair them the best you can (with the spares and supplies you have on board and skills you have developed), and then put things back in order.

In the words of the ISAF Offshore Regulations, "Yachts must be completely self-sufficient for very extended periods of time."

Safety Equipment—A useful safety-equipment checklist is on page 157. Don't be overwhelmed by the length of the list, but consider what type of risk each piece of equipment is designed to address, and consider how this would affect you and your crew.

A personal AIS MOB unit attached to your life vest will automatically mark its GPS position and sound an alarm on every AIS-equipped chart plotter within its several-mile range. An equivalent personal EPIRB has a worldwide range, but the signal cannot be received on board, and there will be a delay for the MOB position to be relayed to your boat via your satellite phone.

still need USCG-approved PFDs on board for an inspection). We attached a personal AIS man-overboard (MOB) unit (aka personal locator beacon, or PLB) to our life vests (see image). AIS is explained in more detail on page 142. Also, you'll want a life raft and a mount/stowage for it so it can be launched quickly. Note that your dinghy is *not* a life raft, although you may consider it a backup if your life raft fails.

Your boat's Emergency Beacon (EPIRB) may be your most reliable method of signaling for help in an emergency (followed by a satellite phone and a single-side-band radio, or SSB). Be sure that all the safety equipment is sufficient for the size of crew you intend to have on board for long passages and is in good repair and properly serviced.

When choosing spares, you'll start with a basic list that includes sail repairs, spare halyards, and rigging parts. Next, consider what's likely to fail on your boat. If the engine's older, you'll want to carry more engine spares. If your boat is heavier (as *Celebrate* is) you'll want to carry autopilot spares.

Navigation—When you're offshore, you'll most likely be navigating by GPS. Whether you use electronic or paper charts, the most practical means of knowing where you are and your speed over ground (SOG) and course over ground (COG) is to look at the GPS readouts. Because of the crucial nature of knowing where you are, carry several backup GPS units. On *Celebrate*, there are GPS units in the chart plotters, and we have a handheld as a backup that we also use for dinghy trips. Also, you can get GPS apps for your smartphones so they can be pressed into service when needed.

Communications—We often use our cell phones for shoreside communications when we're at the dock or at anchor. Further at sea, you have a number of options for communications. Rather than go through every permutation of communications devices, here's what we carry on *Celebrate*.

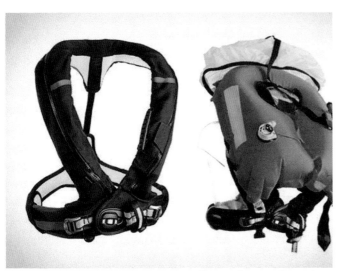

Get life vests that are comfortable so you'll actually wear them. These Spinlock vests have integral tether attachment points and leg straps so you can safely use them to tether up. From spinlock.co.uk.

Note that coast guard requirements are a bare minimum for inshore or coastal sailing, which is inadequate for offshore use. Instead of the big orange USCG-approved personal flotation devices (PFDs), you'll want offshore-rated self-inflating life vests with an integral tether point, spray hood, and leg straps (some of these are not USCG approved, so you'll

The main VHF has a masthead antenna with the main control at the nav station and a remote microphone/control in the cockpit. For longer-range communications, we have an SSB with a Pactor modem connected to a laptop for e-mail (via SailMail). This is important for getting weather information and communicating with other boats over distances greater than the 25-mile VHF range. SailMail has established a worldwide array of shore stations that can be contacted by SSB. SSB data rates are very slow, seldom exceeding 3,000 characters per minute, so messages will be necessarily short.

Watch Commander timer by sail-safely.com is great for long watches.

SSB communications are always hit or miss, depending on the time of day and your position relative to the station you are calling, so we back that up with a handheld sat phone (our installed sat phone system failed even before we started our world circumnavigation). Although it was seldom useful to us for voice calls, we used the sat phone for e-mail when the SSB did not connect.

A Yellow Brick sends GPS tracking information via iridium sat phone technology to draw nice maps and allows messaging too. See ybtracking.com. The Yellow Brick service was the source for the image of Cele-brate's *world circumnavigation track on the cover of this book.*

We also carried a Yellow Brick satellite tracking unit. Although we didn't use all the features of the Yellow Brick, it can also be used for text messages and other communications.

Many areas have "cruisers' nets," which are radio forums on either SSB or VHF. These can be valuable sources of information on weather and other hazards during transits as well as local entertainment, restaurants, and activities while in port. For example, we had a boat transiting ahead of us warn us of unlit boats, logs, and other hazards to navigation.

TIP: Before you start out, be sure your cell phone is unlocked so you can install local SIM cards from other countries. Contact the cell phone provider for details. Also, most countries only support GSM-type phones.

TIP: Noise-reducing headphones make it much easier to hear and understand the SSB, particularly if the engine is running.

You'll Be Sailing 24-7

Watch Schedule—When you're at sea, you'll keep the boat moving. This means you'll need a watch rotation that maintains an adequate lookout at all times. To see what watch schedule works for you and your crew, try a number of different schedules.

Here's what we did on *Celebrate*: With only two people aboard, we would swap 6 hours on and 6 hours off 24 hours per day. We liked having a consistent schedule, with Cathy on from 11:00 to 5:00 and me from 5:00 to 11:00 (both a.m. and p.m.). When we had a third person aboard, we'd go to a 4-on, 8-off schedule. Together we concluded that:

❶ The off time for sleeping was a more compelling part of the watch schedule than the on time. We both prefer a minimum of 6 continuous hours for sleep.

❷ Rotating the watch did not seem worth the negative impact it had on the sleep schedule.

Autopilot—To make the watches easier you'll need an autopilot. We can hand steer for a short period of time, but hours at the wheel are too fatiguing for the short-handed crew. Unless you have sufficient crew for one-hour or two-hour steering stints, you'll be relying on the autopilot most of the time.

Staying Alert—On *Celebrate*, we have a Watch Commander, by SailSafely (one of the few specific products we suggest). It reminds the helmsman at a preset time interval to check the boat and reset the timer. If not reset, a loud alarm will wake the off-watch crew. Many cruisers use a kitchen timer to remind the helmsman to look around every

10 minutes (for example), but it doesn't have the alarm feature. The Watch Commander is particularly valuable for night watches, but we use it 24 hours a day.

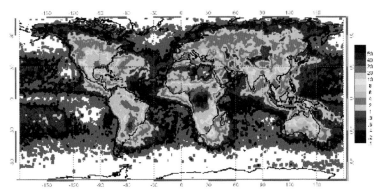

This NASA map shows lightning flashes per year per square kilometer. In midocean, years pass without a lightning flash, and ground strikes are even less common.

Ocean passages can be tedious, and the on-watch person needs to be present and aware in the event of wind changes, traffic, upcoming weather, etc. We set the timer for 15 minutes, so every 15 minutes the on-watch person checks the instruments, adjusts the autopilot course if necessary, scans the horizon 360 degrees, checks the radar, looks at the sail set, etc. Then the watch person can read in the cockpit or occasionally go below to get a snack or go to the head, knowing that the timer will be a reminder for the next look about.

Nighttime—If you're sailing 24 hours a day, roughly half your sailing will be in darkness. Reefing, sail trim, and repairs will not necessarily wait for daylight.

Here's one area where a few low-cost changes can make a great improvement in safety and convenience. Get red/white headlamps and add red/white cockpit lights so you can see control lines in the cockpit. Also, mark reef-points on your halyards or furling lines.

TIP: Mark the lines as well with whipping that you can feel in the dark.

On *Celebrate*, we have great spreader lights. If you need to do something on deck at night, with the spreader lights, it's like daytime. In Fiji, we added a spreader-light switch in the cockpit as well and instituted a new rule: any trim change whatsoever and you must turn on the spreader lights. That way you could check that everything was clear (like the boom and whisker pole not against the shrouds, a lazy genoa sheet not fouled, etc.) before changing the sails. Before the cockpit switch was installed, one might have thought it was just too much trouble to go below, turn the

lights on, make a sail-set change, and then go below again and turn the lights off.

You still need a spotlight to see the sails above the first spreader, but many potential problems are at boom level. For spotlights, we use very high-intensity LED flashlights. These will fit in a coat pocket and are just as bright as many of their larger cousins.

Offshore Navigation Aboard

GPS will be your primary means of knowing your current location, SOG, COG, etc., whether you use electronic or paper charts.

Electronic Charts—You'll most likely have electronic charts aboard, whether in a dedicated chart plotter or just an iPad, and open-ocean navigation can be straightforward. You choose a course to your destination and head in that direction for days or weeks at a time. Sometimes you have an intermediate waypoint or two to avoid a reef or to pick up some favorable currents or weather.

Paper Charts—In making a decision as to whether or not to carry paper charts in addition to the electronic charts here are a few things to keep in mind:

Electronic charting is now *required* on commercial ships, and they are no longer required to carry paper charts, but commercial chart plotter systems must have complete redundancy.

The USCG now considers electronic chart plotter systems to be a replacement for paper charts *if* the chart plotter meets certain requirements of screen size and redundancy. The new interpretation applies only to vessels that carry paying passengers (such as crewed charters). Interestingly, US recreational vessels are not required to carry any charts at all (neither paper nor electronic), although we wouldn't consider going anywhere without some kind of chart.

Using a chart plotter does not eliminate the need to know how to navigate. When you read stories of chart-plotter-caused catastrophes, they are usually actually caused by not navigating properly. If you don't know how to navigate with paper charts, you should take a navigation class even if you go electronic.

Lightning is an often-cited concern about electronics aboard. However, lightning is a shore-related phenomenon and is exceedingly rare on long ocean passages, as shown on the NASA map of lightning frequency. It is highly unlikely that you will lose all your electronics with a lightning strike while hundreds of miles from shore.

Charts in some areas are not very good. This applies to both electronic and paper charts (as the electronic charts are typically based on the paper). See the chapter "Navigation by Google Maps" (page 151) for an example of how charts in Fiji are only somewhat related to the reef locations. Similarly, if you look at the paper chart covering the passage from Vanuatu to Australia, you won't see any of the intervening atolls or reefs (even the Great Barrier Reef). You have to zoom in electronically or look at the higher magnification paper charts to see the hazards.

Squalls at sea are common, but once you learn to spot them early, you can prepare appropriately.

On *Celebrate*, we carry a full set of paper charts in addition to electronic charts and plot our location twice a day while under passage. The operational navigation of keeping the boat on course is entirely electronic with the chart plotter at the helm. With the GPS-supplied COG vector, we adjust the autopilot compass-course a degree or two every 15 minutes (when the timer goes off) to stay on our desired route.

Automated Identification System (AIS)—AIS is another key component to safe navigation. The AIS receiver receives the broadcasts from ships and similarly equipped smaller boats ("targets") and displays their positions and other information on the chart plotter. If you upgrade to an AIS transponder, your boat will also transmit its position to other ships and boats. With AIS, you will "see" ships as much as 20 miles away, but, as AIS uses line-of-sight VHF frequencies, range depends on mast heights. On watch, you can sometimes watch a ship alter course to avoid you at 5 to 10 miles away.

Although ships may have a reputation for not maintaining a good visual lookout for cruising sailboats, they are usually very good about checking their AIS display. Most AIS displays also show the target's SOG, COG, and the closest point

of approach (CPA) and its time (TCPA). Many times, a distant ship will appear visually to be on a collision course with your boat, but if the AIS tells you the CPA will be over a mile, the AIS is correct as long as both vessels maintain course and speed. The AIS also displays ships' names, so it is much easier to hail them on the VHF if passing instructions are needed (or just to say hello if it's been a week since you've seen another vessel).

Weather Gets Worse Sometimes

You should always check the weather predictions before setting out, and if your trip is only for a day or two, you might choose to wait until conditions are favorable. But if you're taking a passage of more than five days, weather predictions become less accurate. Accordingly, choose to sail in seasons when good weather is likely, and most of the time you'll have a pleasant trip.

At sea, get daily weather information via SSB, WeatherFax, or sat phone. Sources of weather information include GRIB files (see below), surface analysis charts (typical weather maps), and a host of other information. You may subscribe to a weather-routing service for daily updates. If you use the SailMail SSB service, it includes a convenient way of downloading weather information.

GRIB files are available free from NOAA and SailMail and other programs and include an easy system for selecting the data you'd like to download, including the area on the earth (a rectangle defined by two corners' latitude and longitude), the simulation model (several weather or current modeling programs are available), duration (days of forecast), etc. With experience, you'll balance the amount of data versus the time it takes to download and longer-term forecasts are seldom accurate enough to be useful. Once loaded, your viewer program will display wind speed, direction, and wave height, on your own local weather map.

The downside of GRIB files is that they are raw data and do not have the benefit of a meteorologist's experience. Also, GRIBs are not good at predicting tracks of hurricanes and other specific weather features. Downloaded in conjunction with text-based weather predictions and weather maps, they can be quite useful.

All this information is valuable, particularly in looking for approaching large weather features, but it won't give you particular local information, and it will only be accurate in a general sense. Wind direction and speed may vary from predictions, and local squalls aren't predicted at all. There is no substitute for looking at the sky (and wind instruments) to predict the weather you'll sail by. Read a marine weather book or attend a class before setting out.

For those occasions where less-than-great weather can't be avoided, you'll need to be prepared. Here are some ideas:

Install jack lines so that (with the tether on your offshore life vest) you can go from cockpit to bow and stern on either side of the boat while always being attached. Flat nylon webbing is better than rope for jack lines. Use the jack lines even in calm conditions so you'll be used to them when it gets rough.

Prepare your rig and train your crew so that each watchkeeper can reef on his or her own. Getting people on deck just to reef tires everyone out. Reefing is a regular activity, and everyone will have a chance to get good at it.

Make sure you have adequate handholds throughout the cabin.

If you are prone to seasickness, find a remedy that works for you. We use scopolamine patches.

Make sure your sleeping accommodations can be adapted to rough weather. On *Celebrate*, some berths have lee cloths and others are built so you can tuck in safely on either tack. When it's rough, one of us often sleeps in the salon in the center of the boat, where the motion is least.

Learn about rough-weather sailing. Sometimes a small change of course can make a big difference in the boat's motion. In approaching South Africa, we SSB-downloaded GRIB files showing a low approaching a few days out, which would eventually have us sailing close hauled. By changing course somewhat to the south, when the low arrived and the wind changed, we could sail 15 degrees further off the apparent wind for much greater comfort.

Expect big seas sometimes. After some time at sea, a 6- to 12-foot swell can be pleasant and soothing; it all depends on the steepness. Large waves in the ocean are not a problem; steep waves can be—even if they're relatively small. Again, a course change can make a big difference. If you're running downwind and down-swell, the concerns are for waves that might break into the cockpit and waves that might push the stern to the side and then roll the boat. Seas will be quite large and steep before this is a danger.

Sometimes there is more wind. Especially if you're going downwind, it won't be long until 30 knots is a condition you are used to. If you're going upwind, it can be unpleasant (depending on the sea state), so you should be flexible.

Practice your procedure for squalls. With a little knowledge and experience, you can see squalls coming (in the sky and/or on radar), predict how intense they might be by their appearance, and take appropriate action. We track squalls on radar so we know how close they will approach, reef early, and are comfortable with a squall gusting over 50 knots. The good thing about squalls is that even with strong winds, there isn't usually time for dangerous seas to develop. Properly reefed, your boat can probably take any wind you might encounter—sea state is the potential problem.

For more severe conditions, have the correct equipment on board (sea anchor, drogue, etc.), and have a plan on what to do—heaving to for a day is better than wearing out your equipment and your crew.

Plan your menu with rough seas in mind. Plan some one-pot meals that don't require much time in the galley (no slicing and dicing). Plan enough snacks that you won't go hungry if it gets too rough to cook. When it's rainy and rough, a cup of hot soup can be particularly inviting, even in the tropics.

Even in good weather, the sea may be rough enough that you can get banged up. Be prepared with a first aid kit and first aid training.

We encountered our worst weather on *Celebrate* near Cape Hatteras before embarking on our world circumnavigation. On one trip, the predicted scattered squalls happened to assemble into a massive thunderstorm, and we experienced winds over 50 knots for two hours. We ran-off downwind (which was offshore) and made the distance back later. On another occasion, we were in the anchorage at Cape Lookout (about 70 miles southwest of Cape Hatteras) when we encountered a few gusts that topped the wind-speed gauge at 99 knots. In this case, *Celebrate* ran downwind at over 8 knots under bare poles. Fortunately, again, at Cape Lookout, we were protected from rough seas.

Another thing to keep in mind is that conditions typically go from nice to uncomfortable long before they become dangerous to the boat. A well-found boat can cope with conditions that the crew cannot. But just because the boat remains afloat doesn't mean that all is well. If rough conditions injure a crew member, this can become a serious problem.

Sailing Will Be Downwind

If you have a light-air downwind sail, such as a cruising spinnaker (or "gennaker"), it's difficult to rig it for single-person operation. We have a gennaker with a snuffer sock, and it can be single handed as long as the wind is light and the water is calm so everything works smoothly. Deploying the sail is usually just fine, but if the wind builds and you want to bring it down, there can be complications. Often, the gennaker stays filled and the snuffer cannot be pulled down, so a correction in the boat's course is needed. This is easy if you have a foredeck person and a helmsman but very

Here's the whisker-pole end showing the stabilizing control lines. The pole lift holds the pole up while the fore- and afterguys (blue lines) prevent fore and aft motion. The genoa sheet hangs loosely through the whisker-pole jaw, waiting for you to sheet in and sail off downwind.

inconvenient for a single person running back and forth. Accordingly, with only two aboard and single-person watches, we do not use the gennaker as often as we might otherwise.

One alternative used by several catamaran captains we know is to use a "heavy-weather" spinnaker, which is smaller and made of heavier material. It can be left up in most downwind conditions, and some use it as their primary sail, seldom unfurling a mainsail.

Poled-Out Genoa—We use a poled-out genoa more often than the gennaker. The secret here (which we learned in a seminar by renowned ocean meteorologist Chris Tibbs) is to rig the whisker pole with three lines—pole lift, foreguy, and afterguy (see picture)—so that it will stay in one place on its own. With no genoa flogging around, one can go to the foredeck and spend plenty of time getting the pole rigged and positioned properly with the genoa sheet through the pole jaw. Now, from within the cockpit, you can unroll the genoa and sheet in, and the sail will fill wonderfully. If a squall approaches, you can roll the genoa up again and leave the pole in place, so when the squall passes, you can just unroll the genoa out to the pole again. If you need to, you can even bring the genoa to the other tack and leave the pole in place until it is convenient to go onto the foredeck and bring it back in.

TIP: To reduce chafe, when you do deploy the poled genoa, make sure the sheet knot is against the whisker-pole jaw. This way the pole will move with the genoa rather than the sheet sliding back and forth through the jaw.

About Your Boat

A Well-Found Boat—You may already have the boat you plan to sail, or you may be selecting a boat for your passage.

Flying the gennaker is great fun, but we have to keep an eye out for increasing wind, and we seldom fly it after dark.

Keep in mind that almost any well-found boat is capable of ocean sailing. How do you know if your boat is well found? Get a survey, and tell the surveyor about your intentions. Watch the survey in progress so you can learn about the condition of the bottom. Then, when you do your own checks down the line, you can see any changes. Search the designer/model reputation—do you know of other boats of the same design that have made similar trips, for example?

Once you have a sturdy boat and a good assortment of safety and navigation equipment, everything else could be considered comfort and convenience. You can select equipment as space and budget allow—you can choose to go without a watermaker, inverter, and so on and "rough it," or you can go for more creature comforts.

Blue-Water Boat Selection—A heavier boat will usually have a more sea-kindly motion than a lighter boat of similar size. For a given hull shape, almost everything that makes a boat faster tends to make it less comfortable at sea and less reliable. Generally, you get more speed from a lighter weight boat, more sail area, and more aggressive sailing; all three of these reduce comfort and reliability.

A multihull will probably have a smoother ride at a choppy anchorage but may or may not be more comfortable in a rough sea. It may be faster downwind. Also, a multihull will have more interior space than a monohull of similar length.

People have made extensive passages and even gone around the world in all kinds of boats, and each boat has its own strengths and weaknesses. It's important to have the boat you enjoy and are comfortable with. Boat selection is a matter of personal preference and budget, so keep the ideas mentioned above in mind when selecting a boat (and also when toughing out a rough sea or repairing the inevitable breakage).

You May Be Shorthanded

On *Celebrate*, we sail as a couple as much as possible. For longer passages, we had a single crewperson join us to shorten the watch times and to act as a backup in the event one of us was out of action. This turned out to be extremely valuable when sailing from Saint Lucia to Panama, where Cathy was laid low by food poisoning and was incapable of standing a watch for a few days.

Depending on your preferences, you probably won't have two people together on watch unless you have at least six crew people on board. Therefore, it's best if you can rig your boat so that it can be handled by just one person on watch in most cases. To accomplish this, you'll want to consider bringing lines to the cockpit so that reefing/unreefing and all sail trimming can be done without leaving the cockpit.

Celebrate, being a somewhat larger boat with nearly 2,000 square feet of sail area, has a considerable amount of gear to let her to be sailed by a single person on watch. The genoa is on a power furler, and the primary winches are electric as well. The genoa can be furled by easing the sheet and pressing the button to roll in the sail. This is fine as long as we are far enough off the wind that the fairlead position isn't critical. If the fairlead block needs to be moved, the forces on the sheet are great enough that the fairlead will

not budge unless the genoa is furled entirely. On many boats, you need only to luff up a bit to ease the pressure on the sail, but on *Celebrate*, if the genoa flogs at all, the forces on the sheet make it dangerous to be on the side deck.

Again, because it is a larger boat, *Celebrate* has in-boom furling by Leisure Furl (Forespar). There is a knack to using it, but it does allow Cathy to reef on her own single-person watch. In order to use the furler, the main must be completely depowered, as it is actually sliding in the track, and with any wind on the main, the luff rope binds in the track and risks damaging the luff tape. If you're going downwind, you don't have to turn the boat all the way around, though. If you sheet in the genoa tight while leaving the main out, then slowly bring the boat across the wind, the backwind from the genoa will make the main luff while still providing drive to the boat—and going generally in the right direction. You can reef/unreef as needed, fall off to the desired course, and sheet the genoa back out.

Planning for a Maintenance Budget

Repairs—Another side effect of running a boat 24 hours a day is that most boats aren't built with that in mind. In the United States, an average boat is used fewer than 100 hours a year. At sea, you'll use it that much every four days. In our

A light-displacement catamaran has lots of interior space but a bumpy ride in rough seas. Here our friends on Folie a Deux are taking the photo on the left.

At 33 tons, Celebrate *is a heavy-displacement blue-water boat with a comfortable ride but needs more wind to get up to speed.*

travels, we never met cruisers who weren't concerned with equipment breakage and repairs.

Chafe is a common problem on a long passage, and we had chafe on the main halyard at the masthead. After we learned about it, we'd lower the mainsail every few days and cut a foot or two off the end of the main halyard to move the chafe point and raise the sail again. We continued this process until we could get a rigger to correct the masthead problem. It didn't take long to conclude that eye splices on halyard shackles, although they look great, aren't necessary, and if you have a chafe problem, you have to cut much more off the end of the halyard if it's eye spliced. Now we use bowlines.

Budgeting—Blue-water sailing will be more expensive than leaving your boat at the dock; there is just no way around it. As you use your boat, parts of it wear out and need to be repaired and replaced. You will also use more fuel and other consumables.

Here's another way to look at it, though: If you have a boat that you sail on the bay and take on cruises for a few weekends a year, you might actually be sailing your boat (hypothetically) 100 hours a year. If your maintenance costs are $10,000 per year for this level of activity, then you are spending $100 per sailing hour. Great news! If you put 2,500 sailing hours on your boat in a single year (15,000 miles), your cost per hour will go down dramatically.

Also, your costs will depend on a number of factors. What is the current condition of your boat? Do you do most of the work yourself? How hard do you sail your boat? How careful are you and your crew, and how experienced are they with this boat? For example, it may be a matter of sound and feel to know when there is too much strain on a line.

In general, outside of the United States, labor is less expensive (except for a few places, such as Tahiti and Australia), and boat parts and supplies are more expensive because of the air freight, duties, agent fees, etc. You can find people to do routine maintenance in many ports worldwide. There are many diesel mechanics who can fix common engine failures—particularly if you have a Yanmar or other widely used engine. You can also usually find craftsmen to do fiberglass repair and woodwork. You might have more difficulty with electronics and watermakers, for instance. In many third-world countries, you can have mechanical parts custom-made at lower cost than you can import replacements. We had a stainless exhaust elbow custom-made in Mexico for much less than the cost of the Yanmar part (which couldn't be imported anyway).

Keeping a happy crew is key to an enjoyable cruise. Crewman Andy Barrow and Captain Charlie have just arrived at Panamarina for an oustanding dinner.

Lastly, Choosing Crew

You'll be in close quarters aboard, and crew selection is likely to be the biggest decision you have to make regarding your safety and enjoyment aboard. On a day trip or short coastal cruise, where the captain is fully in charge the whole time, you can work with almost anyone. The blue-water cruise is different:

- For considerable lengths of time, you'll be in close quarters with your crew.
- You'll be trusting the operating of your boat to your crew.

Crew may be your spouse, other family members, friends, or strangers recruited from other boats or the Internet. But you need:

- People who can be responsible for the boat.
- People you can get along with and like to have around.

On any long voyage, you'll want to choose your crew carefully. In our world circumnavigation, we saw several instances of captains unhappy with their crew, crew unhappy with the boat, crew changing boats, etc. Some of this relates to the close quarters of a sailing boat and the timing involved. Also, sometimes crew inexperience and/or negligence led to friction.

Crew Size—An initial decision is how many people you will want on board. Usually, blue-water watches are hours of inaction interspersed with short bursts of activity. As mentioned previously, on watch, we check up on things every 15 minutes. Even then, everything is often just fine, and no correction is needed. Over time, on shorter initial voyages, you'll learn the watch schedule you're comfortable with, and this will dictate the minimum number of crew you feel you need.

Some captains choose to have a crew of six or more to create a more comfortable watch plan, but it comes at the expense of personal space aboard and a significant increase in provisioning effort. The choice is yours.

Experience?—Energetic, cheerful crew may be better than outstanding sailing résumés. Either way, new crew need to be educated on exactly how your boat works, your safety and navigation equipment, and what is expected of them.

Unique Personalities—Sailing around the world or taking any blue-water passage is not a mainstream activity. People willing to embark on such an adventure are not run-of-the-mill people. Knowing in advance that people are different, it is unrealistic to think they are different only in taking the blue-water passage, but "ordinary" in all other respects. People on blue-water passages are individualists and have their own unique ideas, abilities, and habits. On a passage longer than about a week, people's little habits may begin to wear—particularly for people who are not used to coping with roommates.

Setting Expectations—Many crew-related issues can be headed off by setting expectations. It is important for the captain to decide what is needed from crew members and write it down in advance to share. Do you just need someone to keep watch? Will you need someone to do repairs? Will they be expected to cook? How many meals? What will the menus be like? What will their responsibilities be when you are in port or at anchor or at the dock? What is the alcohol policy?

Set expectations as you see fit. On *Celebrate*, we had a relatively successful crew experience, and the expectations we spelled out for crew joining during our circumnavigation are on page 161.

In Conclusion

This chapter has covered a variety of blue-water topics. With preparation and forethought, you can make your passages fun adventures and avoid many of the potential mishaps. We've covered the primary differences between a blue-water passage and a coastal cruise or afternoon sail on the bay.

Your first blue-water passage may still feel like sailing "off the edge of the world," but, armed with the knowledge

shared from our world circumnavigation on *Celebrate*, you can start with more confidence.

Happy sailing, and enjoy your passages!

QuickStart to Choosing Your Route and Timing

Where Do We Start?

With limitless possibilities for sailing around the world, how do you select which way to go and when? Choosing the safest and most comfortable route around the world depends largely on the weather. Most cruisers choose warmer climates, sailing downwind, avoiding seasonal areas of storms and hurricanes (called "cyclones" in the Southern Hemisphere), and using current boosts when possible. By looking at the probabilities of good conditions, it is possible to select a route for the safest and most comfortable sailing experience.

Trade Winds

There is a more-or-less continuous flow of air called the trade winds. Because the earth is warmer at the equator and colder at the poles, and because of the earth's rotation, this flow is generally westerly (from the west) near the poles and easterly nearer the equator (as shown in the chart above).

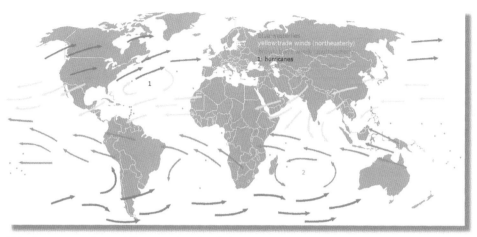

This chart shows the world's general trade wind patterns.

A popular circumnavigation route (starting at the Panama Canal) follows the trade winds west across the South Pacific, north of Australia, across the Indian Ocean south of the equator, around South Africa, and back across the South Atlantic, as shown by the satellite track of our circumnavigation in *Celebrate*.

Note the large area of westerly wind in the far southern latitudes. You'll find most round-the-world racers taking advantage of this wind and rounding the world eastbound instead of the more cruiser-friendly westbound. This far

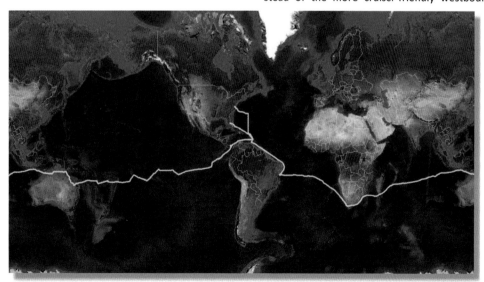

By following the route and timing we did, you can minimize the risk of unpleasant and dangerous weather, but you can't completely eliminate it. This map shows our satellite track following a popular route.

southern route is doable but is likely to be rougher, colder, and less pleasant along with being faster.

Avoiding Cyclones/Hurricanes

Most cruisers avoid hurricanes by staying out of the areas of the world at times when hurricanes are most likely to occur. Hurricanes are powered by warm ocean waters, and the water is warmest at the end of summer. The worst major hurricanes/cyclones will occur in the Northern Hemisphere from July through October and in the Southern Hemisphere from December through April (although dangerous storms can and do sometimes occur outside these periods!). As shown in the storm track map to the right, there are few cyclones at all in the South Atlantic and the eastern South Pacific.

A suggested timing for the route described is to depart Panama in early February, arriving in French Polynesia as the cyclone season closes down at the end of March. Then, the direct route is to proceed through the Cyclone Zone (stopping along the way) to arrive in South Africa in early November before the start of the next storm season in the Indian Ocean. One then crosses the South Atlantic in mid-January, early enough to get to the Caribbean and leave again prior to the start of its hurricane season in June. This "one-year" circumnavigation takes about 15 months and may sound like a rigid and speedy schedule, but in reality there is considerable time and flexibility for sightseeing. For example, rather than spending four weeks in French Polynesia, you might choose to stay longer there and spend less time in Fiji.

In order to have more time in the South Pacific, you might choose to spend a summer (December–April) in New Zealand. Note that to stay in sync with the storm seasons, any significant stopover adds a year to the circumnavigation route. By planning to spend the extra year, you don't have

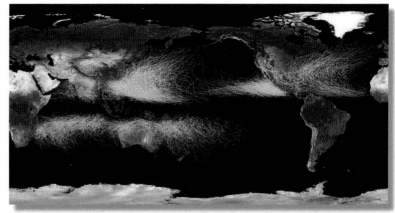

Storm tracks for 1950—2005 showing that hurricanes/cyclones cluster in specific ocean areas. Image by NASA.

to be in New Zealand until November, and you have an extra few months in the South Pacific.

Some sailors choose to risk the storm seasons and plan on safe harbors and/or outrunning storms, as demonstrated by the large number of boats that spend summers in the Caribbean. This is OK as long as one understands the risks.

Caution: Since hurricanes are powered by warm ocean water, increasing overall ocean temperatures are changing hurricanes. As waters warm, you should expect:

- More hurricanes
- More intense hurricanes
- More out-of-season hurricanes

This expectation is borne out with recent devastating South Pacific storms ("Pam" and "Winston") and two Northern Hemisphere hurricanes in January 2016. Mariners must remain vigilant about storms—even out of season.

Ocean Currents

Ocean currents generally follow the trade winds, so as long as you're going downwind, you'll usually get a boost. You can now get up-to-date ocean current information online at:

http://www.oscar.noaa.gov/
(Then click on "Data Display & Download")

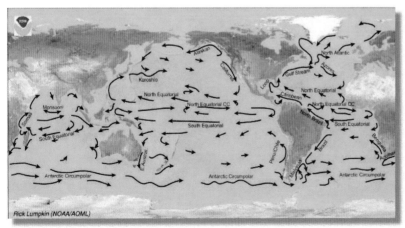

A chart showing the world's major ocean currents.

Navigation by Google Maps

Navigation

We all use charts for navigation, either paper or electronic, but we have found that charts come in varying degrees of accuracy. The further you get from ports used by ships, especially in third-world countries, the less accurate the charts become. This is independent of whether you choose electronic or paper charts, as the electronic charts are usually based on the paper charts. In far-flung areas, there is usually only a single underlying marine survey (except in the Bahamas; see the "Experience Example" on page 153).

The common wisdom is: "The prudent mariner will not rely solely on any single aid to navigation." Sometimes the charts themselves are the "aids" not to be relied upon.

In areas of lower-quality charts, there are times when Google Maps (or Google Earth) can be a valuable addition to your arsenal of navigational tools by showing the exact locations of reefs and other near-surface features.

An Example

In Fiji, charts are reasonably accurate when entering major harbors used by commercial ships. When going to less-traveled islands, the locations of land areas are represented with reasonable accuracy, but the positions of reefs are only somewhat related to their actual positions. Musket Cove is a popular anchorage in Fiji, and while we were anchored there, a large catamaran grounded hard on a reef. They were lucky and sailed free on the next high tide. While it is recommended that you sail reef-strewn areas only in times of good lighting, this is not always possible.

The image below shows the electronic chart of Musket Cove overlaid with the Google Maps satellite photograph. Notice that while the land is represented accurately on the chart, the reefs are only marginally accurate, particularly in the center, where my anchor position is marked on a green reef. In actuality, we were anchored in over 40 feet of water in the center between the two reefs as shown by Google. In this case, Google is the more accurate position source.

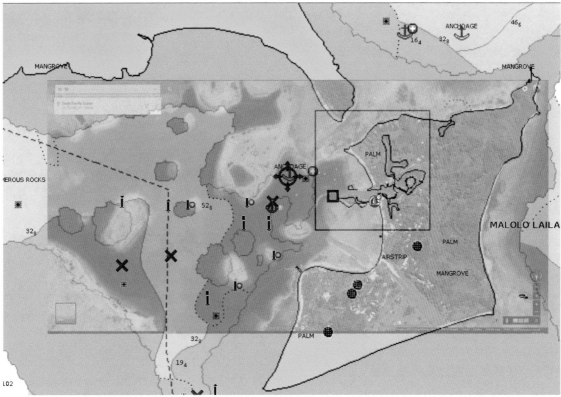

In this overlay image of both a nautical chart and a Google Maps satellite image, note that land areas align, but reefs near the anchorage do not.

Useful Techniques

For this example, go to Google Maps and use only the satellite image mode. You can change from street maps to satellite images with an icon in the lower left corner of the Google Maps window, as shown in the screenshot below.

If you already have a waypoint or latitude/longitude information from a chart or chart plotter and want to see it in Google Maps, enter the coordinates directly into the Google Maps search box ("1" in the figure). Google Maps is quite

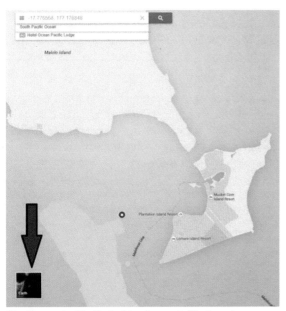

Use the control indicated to show satellite imaging.

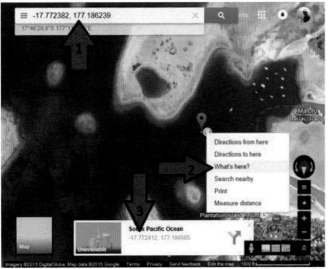

The locations of controls used in Google Maps.

forgiving about the format for input. A decimal-degrees input is shown, but you can use degrees-minutes and put in a space for the degrees symbol like this—"17 46.623s 177 11.038e"—and Maps takes you to that location and puts a marker there.

To find the true position of a feature you see in Google Maps (such as a reef), put your cursor on the feature, right click, and select "What's Here?" ("2" in bottom screenshot). A popup will appear showing the coordinates ("3" in the screenshot):

$$-17.772412, 177.186565$$

Google Maps displays a decimal-degrees system (rather than minutes) and uses minus signs to indicate the Southern or Western Hemispheres. Conversion to decimal minutes positions is pretty straightforward. To get the minutes, take the decimal part of the coordinate and multiply it by 60.

$$0.772412 \times 60 = 46.34472 \text{ and}$$

$$0.186565 \times 60 = 11.19390$$

So the latitude/longitude is:

$$17°46.345' \text{ S } 177°11.194' \text{ E}$$

These coordinates can be keyed into a chart plotter or plotted on a paper chart.

TIP: If you click on the coordinates in the popup, Google Maps will center on that position, and the coordinates will appear in the search box. You can copy-paste from there to your calculator app. Google Maps also does a conversion to latitude/longitude, but it is converted to degree-minutes-seconds, which most chart plotters won't accept.

Plan Ahead

When you most need the Google Maps data, you probably won't have Internet access. Before starting a passage, go to Google Maps and save the information you need about your destination. An easy way (in Windows) is to use your browser to display the map you want to save. Press Alt-PrSc ("Print Screen"). This copies the map data from your browser to the clipboard. Open your favorite image program, and paste the image in. We paste images directly into our word-processing app because it handles images well and we can easily add notes. You can make the images small in the word processor and still zoom in when you need more detail.

Keep in Mind

Even though Google Maps can show you the locations of dangers, it doesn't have depth information, and it can never show you safe locations. Always check your chart to see water depths.

Experience Examples

Our chart plotter uses Navionics charts, which are based on government surveys and are less accurate than the Explorer Charts (which we recommend for anyone sailing in the Bahamas). To reach the Exuma Land and Sea Park from the northwest, a Navionics-charted course will put you on the wrong side of a sandbar, and you'll have to backtrack to get in if you're careful enough to avoid running aground. The sandbar's location is also clearly visible in Google Maps, and, with preparation, you can take a few positions, create waypoints, and sail into the park without hazard.

Similarly, when entering Port Resolution on the island of Tanna (Vanuatu), the charts are sketchy on the location of rocks off the point that you must round to enter the bay. But Google Maps shows the extent of the rocks, because the breakers you'll need to avoid are clearly visible. In some areas, the Google images will be at high tide and/or on a calm day and might not be as useful as the examples here.

All in all, when you're navigating in areas of marginal nautical charts, Google Maps is worth a look.

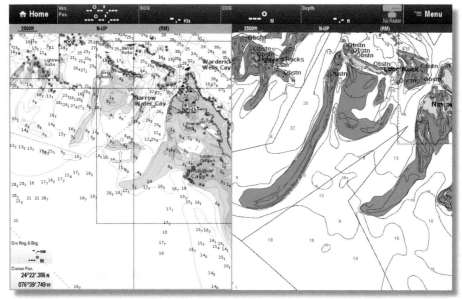

Not all charts are created equal. In this screenshot of Exuma Park in the Bahamas, a chart from a Navionics chart cartridge is on the left, and a chart from a C-Map chart cartridge is on the right. Although they are the same area, the appearance is quite different. More importantly: these charts are from different surveys. From personal experience, the C-Map chart (right) is more closely akin to the actual bottom. The long J-shaped sandbar projecting to the southwest doesn't show on the left but is present on the right and *in the water.*

In this Google Earth image of the same area, the J-shaped sandbar is clearly visible.

A Few Words about Piracy Around the World

What is Considered Piracy?

We are often asked, "Aren't you concerned about pirates?" The short answer is yes, we are concerned about pirates in the same way we are concerned about hurricanes. We take what we believe are reasonable measures to avoid them and then proceed to enjoy our cruise.

"Piracy" can range from pilferage of deck hardware or dinghy theft to the armed attack that ends in cruisers being ransomed or killed. The former is worldwide and unavoidable but can be reduced with basic security precautions. The latter is confined to specific areas of the world and can be avoided (mostly) by not sailing in those areas.

When you hear of "acts of piracy," it's best to dig a little deeper to know what level of piracy is being discussed.

Basic Security

Basic security aboard should dramatically reduce your incidence of problems. The idea is that most minor piracy represents crimes of opportunity. A dinghy is on the beach and no one is around, so the dinghy is taken. Burglars may sneak

aboard, but they don't intend to encounter the boat's crew or face any resistance. With this line of thinking, you need to take steps to make your boat a less attractive target to a potential burglar. Joshua Slocum's famous use of tacks on deck to prevent boarding by indigenous South Americans is no longer a practical solution.

You'll want to have latches so you can lock your boat from both the inside and the outside. Break-ins to locked boats are much less common than simply taking fuel cans or equipment that is left on deck.

Keep your dinghy out of the water at night. It's much more difficult to steal the dinghy quietly if it's on davits or even on a halyard at the gunwales. We have had a dinghy stolen, and it was locked to the side of our boat but in the water. Thieves were able to cut the cable.

You need to be able to turn on exterior lights from inside the boat. We've added bright LED spreader lights. Turning on bright exterior lights if you hear any noise can deter casual thievery.

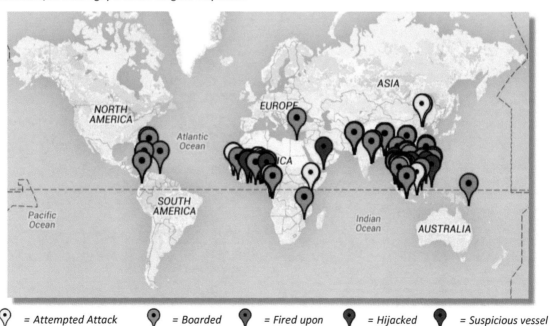

♀ = Attempted Attack   ♀ = Boarded   ♀ = Fired upon   ♀ = Hijacked   ♀ = Suspicious vessel

Reported incidents of piracy are shown as clustered in just a few areas of the world on this map of reported piracy in 2015. Online, this map is "live," allowing you to click on any piracy incident to see the details. For current information, be sure to visit https://icc-ccs.org/piracy-reporting-centre.

Avoiding Piracy

When considering major piracy, our approach is simply not to sail in areas where such incidents occur.

Piracy is bad for tourism, so mostly it occurs only in areas where the governmental authority is weak. In developed areas, government security forces are usually able to prevent piracy altogether. Therefore, if you avoid the western Indian Ocean north of Madagascar, the South China Sea, and some other areas of intense poverty, incidents of major piracy are rare.

Communications and convoys may be the best defense against piracy. If you *do* sail in an area of piracy, stay with a group of boats, and stay in communication if you can. Learn about the security forces that may be nearby and how to contact them via radio or sat phone.

Arming Your Boat

We do not carry firearms aboard, but some cruisers do. Firearms are illegal in many countries outside the United States. They (and ammo) must be declared at check-in to most countries and are often confiscated and then returned upon checkout. Fines for being caught with undeclared firearms may be substantial. Although a handgun or rifle may convey some sense of security, it won't be of much use against an attacker with multiple automatic weapons and rocket-propelled grenades.

However, we have several flare guns aboard, and these are legal in most countries. These are not intended as weapons and do not have much range or accuracy, but they can dissuade a would-be boarder.

Another problem of defending against an armed attack is that the attackers know that an attack is in progress knows their target, and you might not. From your side, identifying pirates can be difficult. The boat coming quickly toward you might just be a fisherman trying to warn you away from his floating net. You won't necessarily know for sure until the attackers are quite near.

Our Advice

Our suggestion is that now is not the right time to cruise the Red Sea, the Suez Canal, the South China Sea, or other areas with a high incidence of piracy. If you do go through these areas, try to go with a group, check security arrangements, and be vigilant.

Outside of high-risk areas, use commonsense security precautions, and accept that crime is rampant in many parts of the world. Some losses are just a part of the cruising experience.

This suspected pirate ship represents the strategy of modern pirates. Operating from a mother ship that gives them great range, smaller boats can be launched to board their quarry. By Chief Information Systems Technician Kenneth Anderson (public domain), via Wikimedia Commons.

Blue-Water Passage Safety Checklist

About This List

This safety checklist is intended for blue-water cruisers and was adapted from the 2015 Transpacific Yacht Race Certificate of Inspection. The Transpac checklist is itself adapted from the comprehensive and interesting International Sailing Federation (ISAF) regulations for offshore races, which is 60 pages long.

Racing regulations are useful, as they have evolved over years of experience. Racers have encountered and documented numerous emergencies and developed equipment and procedures for addressing them. On the other hand, offshore racers press their boats harder and often sail through worse conditions than most cruisers.

Different people have different levels of experience and are comfortable accepting different levels of risk, and offshore sailing is inherently dangerous. Accordingly, skippers may choose to add or omit items. If you are a skipper, you have an obligation to inform your crew of items you have chosen to omit and educate them on items you have added. Similarly, if you are crew, you need to know what safety equipment is on board and what is omitted so you can choose whether a specific voyage is within your comfort zone.

Contact Information

Share this contact information with others before you depart.

Date of Check:

_____

Yacht Name:

_____

Skipper Name:

_____

Offshore E-mail Address:

_____

Sat Phone Number:

_____

Yellow Brick ID:

_____

EPIRB ID:

_____

Yacht Call Sign:

_____

Yacht MMSI Number:

_____

Training

☐ Thirty percent of the crew, including the skipper and watch captains participating, should have recently completed a safety-at-sea course.

☐ At least one crew member should have medical training with at least first aid and CPR certification.

☐ Demonstrate the electronic man-overboard marker by dropping an object overboard, activating the alarm, motoring/sailing out of sight, and then successfully retrieving that object.

☐ In protected waters or at dockside, successfully recover a crew member on board.

☐ For boats with only two crew members, each crew member shall demonstrate recovery of the other crew member.

Below Deck

☐ A durable, waterproof safety equipment location chart should be displayed where it can best be seen, marked with the locations of all safety equipment.

☐ A durable, waterproof through-hull chart showing the location of all through-hulls should be on display where it can best be seen.

☐ A durable, waterproof emergency radio procedures chart showing yacht particulars and calling procedures on radios, sat phone, Yellow Brick, etc., should be on display where it can best be read while using the radios.

Also, there should be:

☐ Navigation equipment *and* charts for this voyage (not solely electronic) and chart plotting equipment.

☐ Emergency water—one gallon per crew member in stout containers or in stout five-gallon jerry cans.

☐ Fire extinguishers, at least two and no fewer than required by the yacht's country of registry, readily accessible in suitable and different parts of the yacht.

☐ Two manual bilge pumps (one in the cockpit near the helm, a second one below deck) with lanyards attached to handles and two buckets with lanyards. Test all bilge pumps for proper operation.

☐ Communication equipment, including a VHF emergency radio antenna.

☐ Softwood damage control plugs of proper sizes, with lanyard attaching them to each through-hull fitting.

☐ A fire blanket adjacent to every cooking device with open flame.

☐ High-powered LED searchlight and flashlights with spare batteries and bulbs.

☐ First aid kit and manual.

☐ Emergency steering tiller.

☐ Tools and spare parts, including a tool capable of cutting the largest shroud on the boat.

☐ Yacht's name shall be on miscellaneous buoyant equipment (life jackets, cushions, life buoys, life slings, grab bags, etc.).

☐ Marine grade retro-reflective material shall be fitted to life buoys, life slings, life rafts, and life jackets.

☐ EPIRB 406 MHZ, tested, with its registration document. Unit shall be water and manually activated.

☐ Storm and heavy-weather sails.

☐ Life jackets for all crew members with retro-reflective tape fitted with thigh straps or a full safety harness, whistle, and waterproof light. If inflatable PFDs are used, they shall be inflated and inspected annually. Service dates shall be marked on each PFD. It is recommended that all inflatable PFDs be integrated with safety harnesses. Inspect cartridges for proper installation, and if over one year old, replace and properly insert new cartridge. Must have the name of vessel or crew member and date of inspection on unit.

☐ Safety harnesses with tethers for each crew member if not integrated into PFD.

☐ All heavy objects, such as batteries, floorboards, and galley stove, shall be secured to prevent coming loose in the event of knockdown or rollover.

On Deck

☐ Alternate navigation lights.

☐ Radar reflector.

☐ Main companionway retaining devices to prevent loss of washboards.

☐ Stainless steel uncoated wire lifelines of proper size.

☐ Cockpit lockers with secure latches for heavy weather and the ability to be locked when the boat is left unattended.

☐ A marine magnetic compass, independent of any power supply, permanently installed and correctly adjusted with deviation card.

☐ A magnetic compass capable of being used for steering that may be handheld.

☐ Two anchors with a combination of the appropriate size chain and rode, ready for immediate use. Shackle pins seized with wire.

☐ Foghorn.

☐ Inflatable life buoys, man overboard modules, or similar type must be certified within one year.

☐ Drogue or sea anchor with appropriate rode.

☐ Jack lines properly rigged and unobstructed on port and starboard sides between bow and stern.

☐ Watertight, high-powered searchlight and watertight flashlights suitable for searching for a person overboard at night and for collision avoidance.

☐ Life raft(s) of sufficient capacity for the crew, packed in a transportable, rigid container or canister and stowed where it can be brought to lifelines or launched within 15 seconds. Life raft must have current inspection certificate.

☐ Each life raft shall be equipped with a grab bag with recommended contents.

☐ "Life sling" style of recovery system with 150 feet of properly sized polypropylene rope.

☐ Man overboard module (buoy with drogue, strobe, whistle flag) not attached to the vessel.

☐ GPS capable of recording a man-overboard position within 10 seconds and monitoring that position.

Pyrotechnic Checklist

☐ Six SOLAS-approved red parachute flares.

☐ Four SOLAS-approved red hand flares.

☐ Two SOLAS-approved orange smoke flares.

☐ Flares stored in a waterproof container along with fire-resistant gloves and eye protection.

Recommendations

☐ Draw boat batteries down; service, recharge, and test prior to use. Test all electrical equipment.

☐ Test radio and sat phone for distance (not with a neighboring boat or in same marina).

☐ Test all electronics aboard vessel.

☐ Service and test all safety equipment, engine, bilge pumps, galley equipment, and marine toilet systems.

Setting Crew Expectations

Whether your crew is made up of friends, family, Internet acquaintances, or people you meet in exotic places, you'll have a more pleasant time if you set expectations before you commit to bringing them on board. Here is the list we used on *Celebrate*, and we believe it helped us have a better crew experience. You can use this list as a basis and modify it to fit your own requirements.

Boat and Crew Expectations

(Start with a paragraph such as this one about yourself and the boat so the potential crewperson has a mental framework as to your abilities, which will influence overall expectations.)

On our voyage, our overall intent is to maintain a happy boat and have fun while having the boat in good repair. *Celebrate* has been continuously maintained and updated and is a comfortable, safe sailing vessel. The boat is extensively equipped, including safety equipment, a watermaker, generator, ice maker, etc., which should make the voyage more comfortable. In brief, the captain, Charlie, and mate, Cathy, together have 100,000-plus miles of sailing experience, and Charlie has a USCG master's license.

The Boat Will:

Provide an environment that is as safe and comfortable as reasonably possible for the duration of the passage to the destination.

Provide breakfast, lunch, dinner, and snacks for the duration of the voyage (meals off boat generally not provided). Crew member might be responsible for special dietary requirements.

Carry additional food to cover unforeseen schedule changes.

Provide an offshore life vest with tether for each crew member.

Provide unlimited fresh drinking water (unless the watermaker fails).

Have ice for cold drinks in port or at anchor.

Provide limited fresh water for other purposes (e.g., short hot shower every day).

Provide a bunk, linens, and towels (some people prefer their own towels and/or a sleeping bag).

Provide a crew-joining letter from the captain to help ease immigration procedures (see end of list).

Pay the costs of fuel and cooking gas.

Pay any immigration fees to enter destination ports.

Pay the costs of maintenance and repairs to the boat.

Provide charts and electronic instrumentation necessary for reasonable offshore navigation.

Maintain ship-to-shore e-mail via SSB (very limited text-only messaging) via a shared e-mail address.

Provide the galley with microwave, propane stove, refrigerator, freezer, etc., for group and individual use.

The Crew Member Will:

Learn the operation of the boat's engine, sails, instruments, safety, and other systems as directed by the captain.

Stand the scheduled watches (with three people aboard: four hours, two times daily) with one person on watch. During his or her time on watch, the crew member will be solely responsible for the safe operation of the vessel. The captain will be available for consultation and will handle difficult navigational situations (docking, narrow passages, etc.). The captain will assign the watch schedule.

Wear a life jacket and tether and operate the Watch Commander timer as directed.

Take appropriate precautions against seasickness.

Participate in some cooking and galley cleanup as needed.

Participate in maintaining the boat.

Arrive at the boat in advance of all scheduled departures.

Have travel insurance to cover unforeseen health or other issues.

Provide his or her own favorite foods in addition to the meals/snacks provided (store in your cabin).

Bring entertainment, such as books, games, DVDs, etc., for his or her own enjoyment or to share.

Not smoke.

Never be visibly intoxicated.

Never sleep on watch.

Maintain his or her living area and head in a seamanlike (neat and clean) manner.

Never bring or possess illegal drugs on board.

Never bring or possess firearms on board.

Provide all travel expenses, including airfare, cab fare, hotel fees, etc., to arrive at the boat at the scheduled time and place and return after the voyage.

Possess a valid passport and any needed visas for countries visited on voyage (some countries require that a passport be valid for six months after entrance).

Crew-Joining Letter

For crew joining you in foreign countries, you may wish to provide them with the following letter. Many countries will refuse entry to visitors who do not possess a demonstrable way of leaving again. For a new crewperson arriving by plane, authorities may request to see an outbound plane ticket, and this letter may help ease the bureaucracy.

_____(Date)_____

To whom it may concern:

I, the undersigned, skipper of the sailing yacht _Celebrate_, registered in the United States of America with a home port of Seattle, Washington, certify that ____(Name)____, passport number _____, is a crew member on the above-mentioned vessel and will be joining the vessel in _____(Country)_____. The above-mentioned person will be arriving with only a one-way ticket, as he will leave ____(Country)____ on board the above-mentioned yacht.

Signed,

Charles J. Simon

Captain of Sailing Vessel _Celebrate_

Suggested Cruising Guides

These are the guides we used on our world circumnavigation, and we thought they were helpful.

General World
Ocean Passages & Landfalls (Heikell and O'Grady)

World Cruising Routes (Cornell)

Pacific
The Panama Cruising Guide (Bauhaus)

Landfalls of Paradise (Heinz)

Pacific Crossing Guide (RCC Pilotage Foundation)

South Pacific Anchorages (Clay)

Charlie's Charts (Polynesia)

Australia
100 Magic Miles (Colfelt)

Cruising the Coral Coast (Lucas)

Torres Strait Passage Guide (Hellewell)

Indian Ocean
Indian Ocean Cruising Guide (Heikell)

South African Nautical Almanac (Morgan)

Atlantic Ocean
South Atlantic Circuit (Morgan)

Atlantic Crossing Guide (RCC Pilotage Foundation)

Havens and Anchorages (Morgan)

Grenada to the Virgin Islands (Patuelli)

A Sailor's Guide to the Windward Islands (Doyle)

Approaches
The Gentleman's Guide to Passages South (Van Sant)

Mexico Boating Guide (Raines)

Suggested Charts

This is a list of charts we used in our circumnavigation. We had a full set of electronic chart cartridges for the trip as well and relied on them for our navigation. We never noticed a significant difference between the electronic and paper charts (as we have in other areas).

Panama

BA 1400	Approaches to Puerto Cristobal
BA 3111	Atlantic Entrance to Panama Canal
BA 3098	Panama Canal
BA 1929	Gulf of Panama
BA 2258	Bahia Buenaventura to Panama

Galápagos

BA 1375	Archipielago de Colon (Galapagos Islands)

Hiva Oa and Nuku Hiva

BA 1630	Plans in the Marquesas
BA 4654	Tahiti to the Marquesas

Tahiti

BA 1381	Approaches to Tahiti and Moorea
BA 998	Makemo to Tahiti

Bora Bora

BA 1060	Huanine to Maupiti
BA 1107	Plans for Society Islands

Niue

BA 4630	Samoa Islands to Southern Cook Islands

Fiji

BA 2691	Fiji Islands
BA 441	Southeastern Approaches to Fiji
BA 1670	Plans in Viti Lehu

Vanuatu

BA 1494	Efate and Plans

Australia

AUS 251	Bailey Islet to Repulse Islands
AUS 252	Whitsunday Group
AUS 26	Approaches to Port Darwin

Bali

BA 946	Ports in Eastern Java, Bali, Lombok, Pulau-Pulau Kagean

Cocos (Keeling)

AUS 606	Approaches to Cocos (Keeling) Islands
AUS 607	Cocos (Keeling) Islands South Keeling

Mauritius

BA 712	Réunion to Mauritius
BA 711	Mauritius

La Réunion

BA 1495	La Réunion North, Pt des Chateaux to Pt de la Riviere du Mat

South Africa

BA 4173	Approaches to Richards Bay
BA 4174	Richards Bay Harbor
BA 4148	Approaches to Table Bay
BA 1846	Table Bay

Saint Helena

BA 1771	Saint Helena

Brazil

BA 540	Baia de Todos os Santos
BA 545	Ports in Baia de Todos os Santos

Grenada

BA 797	Grenada

Saint Lucia

BA 1273	Saint Lucia

Ocean Planning Charts

BA 4061	South Pacific Ocean, Western Part
BA 4051	North Pacific Ocean, Southeast Part
BA 4060	Australasia and Adjacent Waters
BA 4070	Indian Ocean, Southern Part
BA 4022	South America to Africa
BA 4012	North Atlantic Ocean, Southern Part

Caution: In the event of electronic catastrophe, it's always a good idea to have the backup of paper charts. In areas where we do not have official paper charts, we print out chart plotter screenshots of the destination harbors (and alternates). These are for emergency use and are not practical for navigational use.

Index

60946981R00097

Made in the USA
Charleston, SC
12 September 2016